Watch My Rising

Watch My Rising
A Recovery Anthology

37 stories & poems about recovery from addiction

edited by

Lynn G. Carlson

TULIPTREE
PUBLISHING, LLC

www.tuliptreepub.com

*This anthology is dedicated
to every person who walks through the door
of Recover Wyoming's Recovery Center —
to hope and heal and help.*

Contents

Foreword .... *xi*

NEW LIVES

Introduction to New Lives **Lynn G. Carlson** 3

New Songs **Aaron E. Holst** 5

Her Last Haircut, 1937 **Elizabeth Brulé Farrell** 7

De-stigmatized **Pace Lawson** 9

To Give Thanks to Sweaty Palms **P. F. Witte** 17

Tending My Garden **Jean Bonin** 19

Hope **Elizabeth Brulé Farrell** 21

Christmas at the Cayuga Diner, 1970 **Henry Alley** 22

Is This It? **Kimberly Simms** 30

Kissing the Cat **Paul Hostovsky** 32

The Answer Is in Loving Ourselves **Darrah J. Perez** 34

Hi, My Name's Alexis **Alexis Ivy** 40

The Turn I Took **Lucas Zulu** 41

MANY PATHWAYS

Introduction to Many Pathways *Lynn G. Carlson* 45

Taking On Life *Antonio Sanchez-Day* 47

The Pigeons of Lynn *Paul Hostovsky* 50

Salivate *Caralyn Davis* 53

Raven *David Olsen* 63

Our Better Angels *Maureen Geraghty* 65

Last Call in Aberdeen: 1986 *John E. Simonds* 69

Releasing the Elephants *Karina Muñiz* 73

Anonymous Meets Mona Lisa on the Road to Recovery *Ron Watson* 78

FAMILIES MATTER

Introduction to Families Matter *Lynn G. Carlson* 83

Should We Set a Place for Peggy? *Kristina Cerise* 85

Get Your Ass to Al-Anon *Chelsea Lai* 89

Homeland Security *Margaret Smith-Braniff* 102

Family, Interrupted *Patricia McDaniel* 104

With All Due Respect *Lynn G. Carlson* 112

Chile Roasting Season *A. Z. Roa* 120

He's Sober Today *Sheryl L. Nelms* 130

THE CONNECTION

Introduction to The Connection *Lynn G. Carlson* 135

Lost Gospel *Jim Littwin* 137

Since Leticia Williams Saw Jesus *Patty Somlo* 139

Connoisseur *Rebecca Taksel* 146

The Gift I See *Shane Ronel Crady* 150

Thanking Anne Lamott *Billi Johnson-Casey* 151

Out of the Hospital *Elizabeth Brulé Farrell* 157

Shooting Star or Beacon? *Aaron E. Holst* 158

Reference *Paul Hostovsky* 162

Ghost Story *Tom Larsen* 163

Pledge Week *Wendy Elizabeth Ingersoll* 167

Acknowledgments *169*

Foreword

Thank you for picking up this book.

My journey into sustained recovery happened only when despair became so large that it nearly overwhelmed me. The darkness, sadness, and bleakness that had become my life were, paradoxically, also the way out. It seems to me now that hope was waiting just outside the door—waiting to ignite through a tiny spark of "this time, this time, I am willing to do anything to survive."

Miracles of recovery are all around us. The sickness clears, the memory returns, the shakes abate, but our lives are in shambles—recovery begins.

It is estimated that 24 million Americans are in recovery. The New Recovery Advocacy Movement, in which Recover Wyoming (RW) participates, is involved in an effort to change attitudes about recovery from addiction.

This anthology is our way of sharing, and celebrating, the stories of addiction and recovery: dark and light, despair and hope, disease and wellness, imprisonment and freedom. These are stories we hear every day at RW, and we never get tired of listening.

Every day a person seeking recovery arrives at the door of the Recovery Center and is met with a friendly greeting, complete acceptance, heartfelt support, and, of course, a cup of coffee or water.

The staff, persons in recovery, and family members who run RW know firsthand the impact of addiction and the struggle of recovery. They are uniquely qualified to reach out to those seeking help, solace, and healing. Staff and volunteers meet each person who seeks services wherever they are in their recovery, and walk alongside them as they take the next step.

RW offers referrals to services in the community and state as well as support for persons experiencing homelessness. All Recovery meetings (where all pathways to recovery are honored) are held on site. People can get matched with a Recovery Coach if they are interested in having a mentor. Chances are they'll be invited to volunteer because RW believes everybody has something to give. The Recovery Center is a safe place to meet new friends who are also committed to sobriety.

Hope lives at Recover Wyoming.

May you find hope in the stories and poems in *Watch My Rising: A Recovery Anthology*. May you join Recover Wyoming and the other 91 Recovery Community Organizations around the United States, Europe, and Canada as we spread the message:

Recovery is real.

—Laura N. Griffith
Founder and Executive Director,
Recover Wyoming

For more information about Recover Wyoming and
the New Recovery Advocacy Movement, visit these websites:

www.recoverwyoming.org

www.facesandvoicesofrecovery.org

NEW LIVES

Introduction to New Lives

Bless being careful. Bless being mine
again, beautiful for the first last time.

—Alexis Ivy
"Hi, My Name's Alexis"

In this section, the stories and poems show the blessings and challenges of living new lives in sobriety. They depict how we, like Aaron Holst, "search for the words to new songs" in recovery, and how we become our true, better selves the way Darrah Perez does in "The Answer Is in Loving Ourselves."

And always, relapse hovers behind, reminding us that we must do the daily work of recovery the way Jean Bonin keeps replanting in "Tending My Garden."

We do the hard work that recovery demands—for ourselves, our kids and lovers, our moms and dads, and, as Pace Lawson shows in "De-stigmatize," we also do it for each other.

The words you will read on these pages ooze gratitude, as in P. F Witte's poem "To Give Thanks to Sweaty Palms." And as Kimberly Simms says in her poem "Is This It?" they also offer a reminder to

Pin forgiveness to your heart, steel yourself
with a prayer, and turn your sober face to the sun.

New Songs

Aaron E. Holst

I answer the door, smell last night's sweat,
catch quick-down eyes oozing hangover.

His toolbox bangs to the floor,
"I hear your garbage disposal just hums,

doesn't know the words!"
"Nor the tune," I add.

Under the sink, he whistles
dry, fuzzy cotton ball notes.

I know his song—swollen,
coughing, gagging throat,

congested, vibrating head
forever trying to tune

night-before harmony of
bar puke and smoke, breath of

line-dancin' damsels gone sour.
The dissonance of drinking

to live, drinking to die—
A tune I no longer carry.

We two hum along, whistle our own ways,
his, for the next binge,

mine, for the words
to new songs.

Aaron E. Holst spent many years in public service as a firefighter and fire chief in Wyoming and Montana. His poetry and prose have appeared in *Wyoming Voices, Chaparral Poetry Forum, Distant Horizons, Sandcutters, Off Channel, Encore, Emerging Voices, Inner Landscapes: Writers Respond to the Art of Virginia Dehn, Voices Along the River, Open to Interpretation: Intimate Landscape, Objects in the Rear View Mirror,* and online at the Illinois State Poetry Society website, *Open Window Review, Clerestory Poetry Journal,* and *Eclectica Magazine.*

Her Last Haircut, 1937

Elizabeth Brulé Farrell

for Amelia Earhart

She sat in the barber's chair
reading the Miami newspaper.

He stood behind her
trimming the nape of her neck,

cutting her bangs short.
A part of her flight preparation.

The scissors displayed behind glass
at the Air and Space Museum

catch my eye, draw me closer
to the fearless woman who was the pilot.

Running my hand through my hair
I think of dear lost Amelia,

how I detoured from my own map
but was lucky and made it back home.

Elizabeth Brulé Farrell says, "There is no shame in what is true, so I write it. Words are a way to transform tragedy into possibility, give shape to experience, and find what is positive."

Her poems have appeared in *The Healing Muse*, *Poetry East*, *The Paterson Literary Review*, *Earth's Daughters*, *Desert Call*, *Proposing on the Brooklyn Bridge*, and others.

De-stigmatized

Pace Lawson

I'm a senior in high school, smoking an exorbitant amount of marijuana and considering it recreational use. So, it makes perfect sense to light up in the car on the way to graduation practice today.

Lighter, blunt, inhale.

My friend and I pull up to the Civic Center thirty minutes late, our eyes bloodshot, our minds muddled, meeting the graduation class of 421 midway through practice.

We stagger through the breezeway, into a crowded auditorium, and everyone hits the pause button, slowly turning their heads to see us—a couple of clueless stoners. Immediately, Officer Riddlesburger, the school liaison, whisks us out the back door.

His hand jerks me by the collar. "What do you think you're doing, Pace?"

"Nothing . . ." I say. There is an awkward silence as I stare at the floor. I glance up and notice there's a perplexed look on Officer Riddlesburger's face.

"Give me your keys!"

I hand my keys to him reluctantly. I'm forcefully seated against the brick and told not to move. Riddlesburger and a school administrator begin rifling through my truck.

Mom pulls up. *Someone must have called her!* She jumps out of the car, her face red and scowling. Everyone stops what they're doing, backing away, as she comes running toward me.

"What the hell is going on here!?" she screams. My mom is one of the assistant principals at the school, and she is obviously deeply disappointed in me at this moment.

Before I know it, I'm back at home, getting yelled at. Mom is holding up a glass pipe that she found in my room. "I'm calling the police, Pace!"

"Please, no!" I say. I've never been to jail before and I begin to get riled up at the thought. My dad's not saying much, so I turn to him and plead for my freedom.

"Shut up, and sit down," he snaps.

I shove him and he tumbles over the couch and rolls onto the floor. I can't believe what's happening. *I just hurt my dad!* In a matter of minutes I'm hauled off in handcuffs, charged with possession of drug paraphernalia and assault on a family member.

The jail is grungy and smells like unkempt locker room infused with neglected cafeteria. Inside it's dark, dreary, and depressing. The only light available is in the men I meet there. Shorty is the first friend I make. He stays in the most prized bunk, off in a quiet corner of the tank.

We spend hours playing chess, Spades, or Uno. As he wipes my pieces off the chess board, his smile reveals gold teeth. I'm distracted from the game and I blame it on his tattooed head. *What's up with that? A tattooed head?* He tells me stories and makes me feel welcome.

A few days into my stay, as I'm finishing my breakfast, Lightfoot squats on the cold metal toilet and proceeds to stink up the tank. I continue to spoon cold grits into my pie hole and grimace at the reviling stench.

"Too bad they couldn't install the toilet more than ten feet from where we eat!" I say.

Before I know it, T-Nut flies off his bunk and breaks Lightfoot's nose with his fist. Lightfoot rolls off the toilet, with his pants still around his ankles, blood streaming down his face. The lesson is—don't use the restroom while a man is eating. I stack my tray neatly on top of the others and walk quietly back to my bunk.

Sure, these men are some rough guys, but they improve my chess game and preserve my self-respect. I take the time to learn everything about their culture—the lingo, the music, the drugs, and the code. Over the next four years, I am arrested ten times. I become like them by choice, immersing myself deeper and deeper in their culture, until it becomes mine.

It's July 5, 2003. Some friends and I set out to have some fun. We drive across town, carrying with us an assortment of drugs, of course. In the middle of an intersection Clark lights an M-60 firecracker and drops it out the left rear window. *Boom!* Everyone in the car jumps.

Red and blue lights fill the night sky. "It's the cops!" I say and order the driver, "Don't pull over—let's try to lose 'em!"

The driver ignores my sage advice. He pulls over. The officers drag us out of the car and line us up for a pat-down.

"Who's got the gun?" the tall officer with a mustache asks.

"We don't have any guns, sir, it was a firecracker," the driver answers.

Three more police cars arrive on the scene. As they begin to emerge from their vehicles, I have a decision to make. I'm tired of getting arrested and losing my freedom over a bunch of nonsense.

I'm making a run for it! I race across a parking lot and into an apartment complex. The officer with a mustache chases me. He throws a huge flashlight at my head in an effort to slow me down. *Thank God he didn't shoot me!*

I see a guy carrying groceries up some stairs. I somehow convince him, between breaths, to help me. That night we watch the police search the complex from his window while getting drunk on Brandy.

The next morning I call Adriana, who was with us the night before.

"They kept asking about you," she says. "They told us that no charges would be brought against us if we gave them your name."

"They know who I am, don't they?"

"Yes." She sounded somewhat disappointed in herself for giving me up.

"Let's go to California." My recommendation comes as if I have some new level of insight.

We pack our things and head out in my truck, with what little money we have left. We arrive in Santa Monica, at my uncle's house, 1,086 miles away, but the only thing I find on the beach there is hopelessness and remorse.

"What are we doing here?" Adriana asks.

"We're starting over, remember? We're going to build a new life here."

"But your uncle won't let us stay at his house. So, where are we going to sleep, and how much money do we have left?"

What have I done!? Should we sleep in my truck, or in a homeless shelter while we look for work? Is this really happening?

"Where's the cocaine?" I ask in a frenzy.

"Pace, we don't have any."

"This doesn't make any sense, does it?" I'm at the end of my rope. I have no money, no job, and no cocaine. I have multiple charges pending, incidents that happened prior to "evading arrest," and warrants have been issued. Adriana and I decide that I'm bat-shit crazy, we go home, and I turn myself in to the authorities.

After spending some time behind bars, I feel like a new man. I'm born again. My parents are so convinced of my transformation that they agree to fund my first year at Midwestern State University, and with great expectation. Now, I'm 21 years old and living in a dorm, 225 miles away from home, not knowing a soul on campus. It's pretty awkward.

I wander around the dimly lit hallways of the dormitory, looking for friendly neighbors. The guys I meet are fresh out of high school and haven't been exposed to the lifestyle I've become accustomed to. So, I understand the odd look on their face when the first question that pops out of my mouth is, "Do you smoke weed?"

Finally, I come across a guy panhandling. I introduce myself and find out that he likes to be called Can't-Get-Right. After he tries to convince me the money he's asking for is going toward gas to get to Milwaukee, I force him to admit that he's a crack smoker. Next thing I know, I'm smoking crack with the guy and selling cocaine to students at MSU. I remember Shorty, the guy that initiated me during my first stint in jail. The lingo, the music, and the code come back to life.

My academic advisor wants to talk about degree plans. I want to become a cartel kingpin. My professors want me to do homework. I just want to get high. *What happened to the fresh start I was so intent on, upon my return from California?* I spend a year at MSU, get arrested twice, flunk my classes, and get expelled for kicking in someone's door over cocaine.

I'm back in Amarillo, having disappointed myself and my family. So, what do I do when I'm feeling helpless?

Where's the cocaine?

I come across an old friend, who I'll call M, who has risen in the ranks of the drug trade and knows the lingo, the music, and the code just as well, if not better, than I do.

Cocaine comes cheap with this guy and he's quick to bring me into the inner circle. *Now, maybe I really can become a cartel kingpin.* I'm diagnosed with testicular cancer and lymphoma, which definitely doesn't quell my desire to get high or my motivation to roar through life in the fast lane. I'm addicted to cocaine, which does not mix well with the chemotherapy.

I show M the central line the doctor installed in my chest for the chemo the day before.

"Damn, that's sick, bro!" he says. His face contorts as if I were a leper or something. "Maybe this will make you feel better." He lifts the lid to an ice chest and inside are a bunch of bundled packages. He gives me a goody bag out of sympathy for my suffering. Maybe that's all he knows.

While going through chemo, I spend months lying around, smoking more marijuana than ever before, becoming increasingly paranoid and delusional due to heavy cocaine use. I come close to death on a few occasions, smiling and waving as it passes me by. I'm thinking I'm already dead. *Is this a dream?*

One day I wake up and realize the cancer is gone. I face the world again with a new hope. After completing chemo and in preparation for surgery to have the central line removed, the doctor asks me a series of questions.

"What, if any, drugs have you used?" he asks coldly.

"I've been using cocaine," I answer honestly, halfway hoping he'll help me.

"Hmmm . . . any prescriptions other than what we've provided?" he asks with no emotion.

The cancer is now in remission, but I'm having trouble making ends meet. So, I land a job on an asbestos-abatement crew, the perfect job for a cancer survivor. I'm desperate to make enough money to cover my expenses, mainly to fuel my addiction. It doesn't matter that I see death in the mirror, a dark, depressed, and gray face that stares hopelessly back at me. I'm just trying to get by. My motivation to be somebody and to make something of myself has become a rotting corpse.

It's a typical day at work. I'm taking frequent breaks to swig on a bottle of whisky and bump some cocaine. On this fateful day, my boss finds me in the bathroom with quite the setup. He fires me on the spot. I'm numb to it, though. I've been fired more times than I can count. I begin sorting through the thoughts that fly through my head. *Where am I going to go? What am I going to do? Maybe I should resign from life and become chronically homeless, binging on cocaine as much as possible!*

As I begin to take that step out into the wilderness, I feel a tug in the opposite direction.

Wait, is that really what you want for yourself? it asks quietly.

Of course not! I don't want to die in the street alone.

What are you going to do? this voice in the back of my head asks.

Maybe I should just die!

Pace, we've done this a million times, the truth whispers. *You've wished for death but never followed through.*

Yeah, you're right. I chuckle and realize how crazy and dark I'd become. I should go to treatment, then.

Before I know it, I'm phoning the treatment center that my probation officer sent me to years before, which leads me to a halfway house in Denton, Texas, a place known as Solutions. We have weekly house meetings where we get beat over the head with the Big Book of AA. Some guy is up at the podium telling his story, describing how he couldn't smoke just one bag. He describes the typical crack cocaine binge that I know all too well.

I can still get drunk, though. I think to myself.

"Hey let's go get some forties," I whisper to a friend of mine, referring to each of us having a 40 ounce bottle of cheap malt liquor.

"I'm down," he nonchalantly replies, as if it's no big deal to drink while living in a halfway house. For goodness sake, we signed a code of conduct acknowledging that we wouldn't.

We're in a mall parking lot drinking and I remember Shorty, the lingo, the music, and the code. I begin to feel somewhat rebellious like, *F*** it! I only get one life and I'm going all in!*

"Let's go get some MD," I suggest, yearning for the cheap wine that's known to provide a quick drunk.

I wake up on top of my friend in an upside down SUV on I-35. The last thing I can remember is making the decision to drive to Irving to get some heroin. I must have blacked out.

"Dude, are you all right?!" I scream. I see blood on his shirt and begin to panic.

"Yeah, man, it's just my arm," he replies as he rolls around trying to make enough space between to two of us, so that we can get out of the mangled vehicle.

Thank God he's alive. I see that his arm is torn up, but all else is intact. I don't have a scrape on me.

I climb out, through the driver's side window, which is directly overhead. I pull my friend up through the widow by his good arm. Sure enough, the red and blue lights have already lit up the scene. They haul us off to county jail and I smirk as the officer takes my mugshot.

I have just enough cash in my wallet to bond out. This life isn't working for me anymore. I contemplate suicide once again, with no real motivation to follow through. Instead, I just pray for death. *God, please take me. My life isn't worth it anymore.*

The next morning I begin walking, hoping that I still have my job striping parking lots. I'm not sure Solutions will take me back, either.

Please help me, God!

Within a split second something in a deep recess of my mind kicks into gear and I begin to feel myself resigning from Shorty's subculture. I give up the lingo, the music, and the code. I had identified with a way of life that was destroying me. Now, I'm letting it go. I feel a sweet release from a bondage that I had previously embraced.

Deep in my gut I feel a burning for something fresh. I'm not sure where I'm headed, but back to a halfway house and a job that may, or may not, take me back. I sense that where I'm headed is much further down the road, though. A sense of newness has overtaken me. If they don't take me back, then I'll still be forging a new life for myself and will inevitably reach my destination.

It's been nine years since that day. I'm 31 years old now, with a wife, three kids, and two college degrees. I'm currently working on my master's degree. I've been working as an LCDC, or drug counselor, for five years in a variety of treatment settings.

Back at the halfway house in Denton, I thought, *Pace, you can open up a place like this one day.*

The idea seemed a little far-fetched at the time, but in November 2014, I founded and incorporated Options Recovery of Amarillo, a 501(c)3 nonprofit corporation. We operate a sober-living home in Amarillo, Texas. The dream I carried with me for nine years has become a reality.

It isn't easy. There are people in my community that don't have any compassion for people with Substance Use Disorders. They deny that such a problem even exists. They recommend the "addict" man-up and roll their eyes at treatment and recovery support services.

The City of Amarillo wants our sober-living home out of the middle-class neighborhood it currently calls home. I hold the letter in my hand that claims we can't operate a sober-living home in that area due to zoning and city ordinance.

I plead with the city attorney, "But you see, people with Substance

Use Disorders are protected by ADA and FHA, and can live together in any neighborhood, in any city in the U.S., according to federal law."

"I see where you're coming from but this decision is above my paygrade," he replies with an unusually flat tone.

I hand him the document I've prepared. "This is a Request for Reasonable Accommodation and I'm prepared to file a complaint with HUD on the basis of discrimination." I keep my calm. I know this is a necessary part of the process.

But file a complaint with HUD? I don't want to be known as the guy that filed suit against the City of Amarillo because they discriminated against people with Substance Use Disorders.

He perks up a little bit. "Hmm . . . I see. I'll talk to the mayor and council members and get back with you by Friday."

We shake hands and I leave his office. I'm a completely different guy today, compared to who I was before. I respect authority. I love my community and the people in it. I have a heart full of compassion and yearn to see people overcome addiction, but I've obviously still got a rebellious streak. I mean, I just stood up to the City of Amarillo!

A few days later I get the phone call. The city officials have granted my Request for Reasonable Accommodation, and we get to keep HUD out of this! The city attorney also tells me that they have to rewrite some of the city ordinances to better accommodate sober-living homes in the future.

I run home and wrap my arms around my wife, Melissa, because I know that at the end of the day, no matter what I do for a living, or how things turn out, for better or for worse, she'll be there to share it with me.

I'm Pace Lawson and I'm a person in recovery. If I can do it so can you.

Pace Lawson inspires people with addictions to hope in a brighter future. As a licensed professional, he's worked in a variety of treatment settings and maintains that there are many pathways to recovery. He is an inspirational speaker and founder of Options Recovery (www.optionsamarillo.com), a service provider for people with Substance Use Disorders. Most importantly, he is a dedicated husband and father of three.

To Give Thanks to Sweaty Palms

P. F. Witte

To be born again
alive
to have risen up
from the ashes, the ash heap
of dead matter
of twilight sleep
from bed that I had slept in
so long, napped, dreamt

the dreams of the pill-taker
the booze swallower
to swallow
the prescriptions, renewals
pints, quarts, colored glass
odd labels
to lie down with them all
until gone
almost gone, my life

in the hollow of a hole
left to lie
and sleep and sleep
body thinned to twilight
palms paled cold
heartbeat unsure,
and to rise

to rise out of this
to crawl and drag and curse
to put down each
pill, bottle, glass
each day
the awakening each morning
to bless my sleep the night before
my drugless, boozeless sleep
to say thank you sun, sky, green tree
to know my eyes awake
clear water washing over
every thing
to have a hand, five fingers
sweaty palms—

thank you sweaty palms.

P. F. Witte was born and raised in New York City. She writes poetry as well as prose. She has won the Allen Ginsberg Poetry Series Award and the Pat Parker Memorial Poetry Prize. She has read with such poets as Adrienne Rich, Audre Lorde, June Jordan, and Sapphire. Her readings have taken her from Columbia University uptown, to The Minetta Lane Theater for the AIDs Theater Project downtown. Her work has been published in the anthologies *Women on the Verge* (St. Martin's Press) and *Women Strike Back* (Storyline Press).

Tending My Garden

Jean Bonin

Fragmented pieces

of my past

congregate together

a huge army

of unruly revelers

an entourage of rebellion

armed and dangerous

they sweep through

the freshly planted

garden of my soul

trampling to death

my carefully tended

tiny green growth

of hope

then when all of

the prisoners

have been taken

and

decency has been defiled

the abhorrent army

will return victorious

to its slumbering pit of hell
and I will once again
plant my garden
and pray that
they sleep well

Jean says, "We could have been any three twelve-year-olds at the playground, the difference was we'd stolen a mason quart jar of homemade liquor. I have never tasted anything quite as awful. We passed the jar between us, chugging hard and fast. It came up a lot faster than it went down. The experience left me sick, dizzy, disoriented, retching my guts out in the dirt. And for reasons I will never understand, it left me wanting more. It left me wanting to feel anything but 'normal.' That is until the birth of my oldest daughter. The road back, although it cannot be minimized, it can be summed up in a few words—a praying grandma—a faith in Jesus Christ—regret that leads to change—midnight poems and prayers—tears too numerous to count."

Jean Bonin has been blessed to have had several poems, devotions, and short stories published.

Hope

Elizabeth Brulé Farrell

I want to write the word
letter by letter
as you would with a stick
in the sand
or a finger in the dirt,
each letter
magnified on the ground.
Four letters
shaped by a shoe tip
or the edge of a rock.
A wish
in wet cement.

Christmas at the Cayuga Diner, 1970

Henry Alley

Serious business, shoveling snow, when the Cayuga Diner has won awards for the best hangover breakfast in the county, and it's Christmas morning, and the parking lot is packed white from the night before. The flurries were fighting me; they descended and covered my fairly light jacket, and underneath, all I had on was an undershirt. Through the flakes: the isolated Christmas tree belonging to the gas station across Miranda Road. It was framed in the window, left on and winking, and winking more because of the snow falling between. My sock hat had gathered a second cap from the blizzard, like the rounded top of a fence post.

Serious business, feeling young and serious and muscular, shoveling so heavy I felt a break in my arms every time I tossed a clump aside. My body was hardened from times in jail, times in prison, two years altogether. I was the result of the reform of a recreational program, created by well-meaning officials, of lifting weights and running around the prison yard. My body was drug-free as well, because I had been bounced, in and out of jail, from one rehabilitation program to the next, and it had finally taken.

Lily, the owner of the Diner, still believed in me, and had kept my job waiting during the full two years I had been away. "You'll come back," she had written on a post card to me in prison. "You come back and work, Charlie."

She was sharp and Filipina and still bearing a spark from fighting President Marcos and his wife. She knew what it meant to hold out. So I shoveled to get the whole lot clean by 10 a.m., when the thickest of the crowd would be getting there, if we could trust history. It was a matter of honor to get done and to get into the beehive of the kitchen, with my sleeves rolled up and my apron on, reaching deep into the stainless steel sink.

There were times when I would get lost, in reflection, wandering on the Miranda Road, with it being completely abandoned and darkness coming, with only the points of the trees on the low-lying hills being visible. I was in that reverie at this moment, just before 7 a.m., with the little highway all in snow and the Christmas dawn just coming up. As I was about to heave the next shovelful, a cardinal came down and perched, like a sculpted red Christmas ornament, on the bough of a blue spruce, knocking snow down on my head. I must have stood like a statue, for a full minute, hoping he would not leave. I had cleared half the lot by then, and when the bird took flight in a beautiful flutter of crimson wings, I turned and saw someone standing there in the part of the lot that still wasn't touched by a shovel. His shoes weren't visible in the drift. He had wrapped himself from head to foot in a coat that looked like a tan tarp, and he had a sock hat pulled down so low over his face he could have been anyone. There was a yellow Lab mix with him, shivering at the end of rope.

"I thought you might be here," he said, pulling the cap up some.

It was Cliff, who had been with me in Elysian Creek Correctional. We had flipped out at the same time, so we had both been in the Williams County psych jail, too.

"Merry Christmas," I said. "I hope you don't mind if I go on shoveling. I've got only a t-shirt underneath, and I need to stay warm."

"I've been out on the road five days," he answered. "And I'm froze all the way through. I've been trying to find a place for me and my dog here, and this dog isn't even mine. Someone just left him at the bridge a couple of nights ago, and I got stuck." The piercingly blue-eyed man with the gray-flecked beard looked at me. "I need a place to stay, man. You and I were pretty tight."

"Yeah, I was expecting to see you in meetings," I answered. "But didn't."

"No, I don't need that meeting stuff. I just need something in my gut."

The restaurant's open sign went on, and a car pulled into the lot. The people in it looked like jolly travelers. The woman had holly in her hair.

The man's face was flushed with Christmas cheer. Tie-dyes could be expected as soon as they got out of the Dodge Dart.

When the car door slammed, the dog, skittish already, made a jump, and Cliff yanked the rope back hard. The dog yelped. Cliff started yelling at him, and the dog cowered all the way down.

"Hey," I said. "Hey, hey."

Lily, stationed at the glass door with windows, made a motion with her hand to shoo this man off the premises. She also made a more complex motion to ask if she should call the cops. Frightened about my probation, I furiously shook my head.

"I don't have any place for you to stay," I said quickly. And like a fool, "I only have a little apartment, which the county subsidizes. There isn't room for another man and a dog."

"We'll take a room anywhere. We're not at the point of being choosey, are we, Andy?"

At that point, the cowering dog looked up and smiled, as yellow Labs do.

Cliff had worked hard at Elysian and even in jail to get his shit together. To stop pot and meth and alcohol by being honest. He'd previously beaten up a man whose home he had broken into to steal prescription drugs. He'd copped to it in group, the way we all copped. We were hard on him the way we were all hard on one another.

Now he was a wayfaring iceman.

"I myself can't help you," I said. "But I'll go in and ask Lily if you can warm up in the shed and I'll bring some food out for you and—"

He spat into the snow while Andy tentatively sat down, his haunches shivering. "I'm not asking for a fucking handout, Charlie," Cliff said. "I want a little space of my own."

I shoveled, more vigorously, but taking care not to scare Andy. "Sorry. Can't help you there. For starters, my probation wouldn't allow it, and next, I don't have room. I hardly have enough for myself."

There was a furnace going on in Cliff's glance. Three more cars came into the lot. Some of the passengers were very merry. Two more looked as if they could use the hangover breakfast, like Cliff. They didn't look as bad as he did, but a few years down the road, they could be on their way.

"You see, Charlie," he said, "you don't have any choice. Either I stay at your place or I'll tell your boss in there all about you."

"She knows all about my gay past, if that's what you mean."

Cliff shot me his furnace glance again.

"She also knows," I went on, "about my straight past. All about Carmen and my daughter. So you can take your blackmail and shove it up your ass."

"I'm not talking about that little stuff. I mean why you were in the slammer in the first place."

I was moving so quickly with my shovel, the lot was two-thirds done, but Lily, having seated the next three sets of customers, was back frowning at the door.

Underneath, I was starting to sweat my t-shirt through. "Obviously you don't read the papers" — still, I didn't want to think about this part of my past — "but there was a whole section in the *Cayuga Journal* on Lily helping me even with my prison record." I started to smile, despite myself. "You'd be telling month-old news."

"Dirty cocksucker," he said. "And in more ways than one."

He yanked on the rope so hard, Andy yelped again. Louder this time.

"Dirty cocksucker yourself," I answered. "Abuse that dog one more time, and I'll knock you into next week."

He dropped the rope and pulled himself up to me. The memory of a shower we had taken together was full on. Suddenly he slugged me in the stomach, and I hunched over. The man had a powerful body still, probably from being a gravedigger for so many years while he was on his way to bottoming out.

I went flat down in the snow. By that time, Lily and Smiley the cook and Smitty and Kip the waiters had come running out.

Cliff hightailed it away, leaving Andy behind.

* * *

Three years ago, a Thanksgiving storm buried the county in ice and snow. It made our new 50-unit complex look like an iced gingerbread house from the early 1900s. Its 30- by 40-foot swimming pool froze over like a tray of ice cream. Later that weekend, a seven-year-old and two six-year-old boys were playing in the snow in the parking lot when they probably dared one another to walk over the ice of the pool. They found a hole in the redwood fence, three slats wide, a hole which the *Cayuga Journal* would be so fond of showing, and crawled right through. They fell straight through the center of the pool and drowned. Someone in the upper units saw them and screamed a phone call to the state police, but by the time they got there, nothing could resuscitate the boys. At first the district attorney didn't file any charges, but after conducting an investigation, he decided that the owner and I, the general groundskeeper, were guilty of criminal negligence. I argued that I had never received a work order, but to be honest, I was so zoned out on drugs then, how could I possibly remember?

The judge gave me two years. After I had been in eleven months, I was transferred to Elysian Creek Correctional.

In dreams, over and over, I saw the snow-topped redwood fence, the snow-covered pool, and the tracks leading across the tentative crust to the eight-foot drop. In every dream, I mended the fence, with about four dollars' worth of materials. I saw the portrait faces of the little boys appearing alongside the photos of the pool and the "culprit path" through the fence. Their faces had all seemed to be caught at a Sunday school class. These dreams were like the failed efforts of the policemen, the firemen, and the medics to resuscitate them both in and out of the ambulance.

I had been allowed to speak my apologies to the parents.

To the grandparents.

It did little good. I had robbed them of their children and their grandchildren and therefore the best of their lives, they said.

I made my plea that in order to support my own child, I needed to work and not go long to prison.

That did little good, either.

* * *

After the skirmish with Cliff in the parking lot, I asked Lily if I could use the shed. It would not do for me to sit on a stool at the back of the kitchen and bend painfully over the punch in my stomach. Also I wanted a place where Andy could stay, since obviously he was my responsibility, for the time being. I ladled a bowl of soup into an old cottage cheese carton, and took it out back. I left Andy in the shed to bolt everything down, while I got a space heater, and connected it to the outlet in the overhanging light. I hoped the circuits wouldn't pop.

Lily came in.

"We get some chicken scraps for you, too," she said to Andy. "But no bones. How's your stomach?" she asked me.

"I can stand up now."

"Good. Oatmeal with raisins for you. Immediately. Come out and get it yourself. We're going to have another three hundred today. Seventy-five-person capacity. That means everybody in and out four times. That means you wash dishes soon, if you can."

"I can," I said. "I just need to change this"—pointing to the wet armpits of my t-shirt—"and I'll be in there like a dervish."

"No, no, you eat first," she said. "You no good to us unless you eat. You ask Smiley for an extra t-shirt. He keeps his own in the cloak room."

I sat with Andy for a while and helped myself to some oatmeal. We watched the snow coming down outside the window, which was damp with condensation from the space heater. When Lily came in with chicken scraps, I said, "Lily, do you have to report this to my probation officer?"

"Probation officer?" She snapped her red-lacquered fingers. "What probation officer? You shut up."

She went out the door, and Andy, who had carefully attended while we talked, got up and started bolting down the chicken. "Easy, easy, friend," I said. "You haven't eaten in a while."

I left, telling Andy I would be back. Outside, the cardinal was busy again, flying from one pine to the next and causing powdery avalanches once more. In the hubbub of the kitchen, Smiley fired out orders in a Santa's hat and yelled over platters of pancakes. I felt a little woozy as I put on my apron over Smiley's t-shirt, an extra-large that was all stretched out in the sleeves and the chest because of his massive size. I filled up the second stainless steel sink, and when I heard a familiar voice, I turned. Through the pass-through, I could see my ex-wife and daughter. We had split custody, and I wasn't supposed to see my daughter until tonight.

I could tell by my ex-wife's jerky motions she had relapsed and wasn't any more sober than Cliff. She wore a knit green beret, and a red sweater on her small, thin frame. My four-year-old Melanie wore the purple coat that was too short for her. In getting ready to sit down, they were throwing off a shower of snow that was melting by their table. I turned the water on, full blast, into the sink and looked down into the well so I wouldn't have to see my ex. I just leaned on the drain board. At a loss.

Lily came into the kitchen, holding her order pad. "That's your daughter out there. Go," she said, pushing me. "It's Christmas. Wish her a Merry Christmas. Here"—she grabbed Smiley's Santa hat. "Wear this. You don't look decent otherwise."

I went out with the water running into the first sink.

First thing Carmen said was, "I need a little money for today."

"Just buy whatever you want here," I told her. "I'll cover it with Lily."

Melanie grabbed my leg.

"I mean money for a few other things," Carmen said.

I looked at her and got a gaze that had gone to the moon. "No, I don't think so," I said.

Carmen bent her head—she always looked as if she belonged in a Modigliani painting. Vulnerable. "I'm a little short on Christmas gifts," she went on.

"I'll take care of that tonight."

"Money, I mean money," she said, standing up. People were looking at us, even the hungover ones. Once again, I felt the punch in my stomach. Outside the window, the cardinal soared from tree to tree, in red arcs.

"Look, Daddy," Melanie said, pointing. "The red bird."

Suddenly, as though she were guided to it, Carmen turned and, in nothing but her skirt and red sweater, stumbled toward the door. I ran after her, and in the lot, with the large flakes coming down, seized her arm. She tore herself away, and unlocked the car. I made a grab for the door and just missed it slamming on my fingers. I slipped, despite my great shoveling job. She turned the wipers on and cleared the windshield, pulling off, with me frozen and nearly flattened again in the lot.

I went back in and I dusted myself off with a paper napkin from Melanie and Carmen's table.

My Santa's hat was topped with snow, like a little extra cotton. The kitchen crew was watching through the pass-through.

"Is Mama coming back?" Melanie asked.

"I don't know," I said, and ushered her to the shed to meet Andy. We sat, all three of us, watching the snow.

Henry Alley is a Professor Emeritus of Literature in the Honors College at the University of Oregon. He has four novels, *Through Glass* (Iris Press, 1979), *The Lattice* (Ariadne Press, 1986), *Umbrella of Glass* (Breitenbush Books, 1988), and *Precincts of Light* (Inkwater Press, 2010). His *Leonardo and I* was winner of the Gertrude Press 2006 Fiction Chapbook Award. In 2015, his story "Yard Sale" won the Gertrude Press Short Story Contest. His stories have been published over the past forty years in such journals as *Seattle Review, Outerbridge, Michigan Quarterly, Virginia Quarterly Review, Clackamas Literary Review, Gertrude,* and *Harrington Gay Men's Quarterly Fiction.* His essays have appeared in *The Journal of Narrative Technique, Studies in the Novel, Twentieth Century Literature, Kenyon Review,* and *Papers on Language and Literature.* The University of Delaware Press published his book-length study, *The Quest for Anonymity: The Novels of George Eliot,* in 1997.

Is This It?

Kimberly Simms

After The Strokes' Song

Those days just after thirty
coming down from an afternoon buzz
on a sunny afternoon in late winter.
Dust motes sparkle in the air
like a thousand worlds disappearing.
The room is orange, full of dissipating sunlight
like a dream, like the stench of a Barcelona street:
beautiful, crumbling, old, artistic, and broken.

Things could never stay that way,
empty and rich, hollow and brimming,
chasing a feeling that was nothing more than a song,
than a poem on the tip of your tongue,
than a night that can never be reclaimed:
achy, languishing, confused, self-sacrificing
on an altar with no purpose or god.

But it was not it. It was just a beginning.
A rebirth on the heels of too many funerals.
Beyond the blood from a broken pint glass,
beyond the nightmares of an aging veteran,
beyond the old man alone in the grocery store line
buying three tins of tuna and a loaf of white bread.

We all have choices to make:
paint the room a new color, beat the dust from the rug,
find the art in a blooming flower bed,
embrace the beauty of your smile in your child's face.

Turn to discover a life you have blown back into
bountiful, orange flames with your breath on dying embers.
This is it. That broken down couch has nothing for you.
The bar at 5 in the morning is black as a coffin,
but the afternoon air is crisp on the highway of rebirth.
Pin forgiveness to your heart, steel yourself
with a prayer, and turn your sober face to the sun.

In addition to her work as a teaching artist and her role as a mother and wife, Kimberly Simms is an award-winning poet. She was recently named the 2016 Carl Sandburg Writer-in-Residence. She was a member of the Greenville Slam Team that won the South East Regional Poetry Slam in 1998, and has been published in esteemed literary journals such as *The Asheville Poetry Review, The South Carolina Poetry Review,* and *Eclipse.* She has been deeply stirred by the struggles of addiction in close family and friends. She formerly worked for a center that provided therapy for teens at risk for addiction. You can learn more about her at www.kimberlysimms.com or on twitter @witsendpoetry.

Kissing the Cat

Paul Hostovsky

In the catalog of my addictions,
which is in the order I acquired them,
the mouth of my cat Pinky is preceded
only by my thumb.

His mouth was the only mouth
that didn't speak the language
of our house and television,
so I knew he'd never tell

as one by one my self-propelled
fish-mouth kisses found his mouth
and exploded, his eyes
dilating like the binocular view from space

of a world going up in smoke,
his ears changing shape like a hat
changing heads on his head.
Still as a water jug he sat

enduring as I sipped his spout
on the lime couch
in front of our television, which
in the catalog of my addictions

would be the third entry.
According to my sponsor Phil,
either we give them up in the order
they're killing us—which is often the reverse order

of their acquisition—or else
we simply exchange them one for another
and they kill us cumulatively.
Pinky died when I was off at college

learning to shotgun beers and roll a joint
while steering a car with only one knee.
I never graduated. But I did finally get sober.
And when I got sober I got a kitten.

He tottered around my apartment, tentative
and awkward as my new sobriety.
So I named him Thumbs. And now we're just
two old toms living together, complacent

and fixed. We've given up everything
including sex. He mostly likes to sit
on the kitchen table next to my cup and my plate
while I'm eating. And mostly I just like

to let him.

Paul Hostovsky celebrated 25 years of continuous sobriety on April 28, 2016, a day at a time. He is the author of eight books of poetry, most recently *The Bad Guys*, which won the FutureCycle Poetry Book Prize for 2015. His poems have won a Pushcart Prize, two Best of the Net awards, and have been featured on *Poetry Daily, Verse Daily*, and *The Writer's Almanac*. Visit him at paulhostovsky.com.

The Answer Is in Loving Ourselves

Darrah J. Perez

The importance of sobriety in my life is what keeps me grounded today. At 35 years old, I've witnessed my fair share of the tight hold addiction has on so many of us.

Losing my father to suicide when I was three years old played a factor in my self-destruction. My struggle started at a young age with drugs and alcohol. I began the revolving door—using to the point of blackout and then ending up in jail. When sober, I would hear from others the violence and stupidity that was played out by me. I knew that the intoxicated, belligerent person was not the same person I was when sober—that scary person was a complete stranger to me.

What makes the violence tick? I asked myself. Why would I drink to the point of not knowing where I was, what was going on, or who I was with? That revolving door got tiresome to me. I vowed to get acquainted with this other person in me. I looked into my childhood, my adolescence, my young adult years. Something was missing, and I wasn't absolutely sure what it was.

I began fixing myself, like a broken clay pot, sealing my pieces together, one by one, with a gold setting. The blame, the hate, the unwanted feelings, all engrained an imprint within my being, but then there was more—the feeling of being born in the wrong body grew stronger and stronger.

At a young age, I remember lying in my bed looking for the part down there, the one I knew for sure must have been sewn shut. I knew deep in my mind that God must have made a mistake. I identified with being a girl so bad that it began throwing major depression onto me.

I remember, getting called names—the names little boys get called for tending to be more feminine. Names like faggot, queer, and sissy. I had long hair, a soft feminine voice. I remember a time or two in public, strangers would ask my mom if I was her daughter. The ring of being called "her daughter" really sang harmonious within my soul.

My grandma once told me I couldn't come into the women's restroom with her anymore. Her exact words were, "You're a boy now! You have to use the boy's bathroom."

As I grew older, I attempted to hide it, and fit in with society's idea of what a boy should be and what was acceptable and unacceptable. I cut my hair really short to make a handsome appearance come out. I deepened my high-pitched voice. I began experimenting with being with girls in sexual relationships. I fell in love a few times, and then I discovered being with girls was not who I was or who I had the real attraction to. I desired being with a man.

The first man I had desires for was 16 and I was 14. We hit it off right away. I met him when I was locked away in a juvenile detention center for a few days. After I was released, we stayed in touch through phone calls and letters. My mom didn't like him. I knew this when I found a lot of unopened letters from him in her desk drawer at work. She would say, "Stay away from him."

When he got out of jail, we never once crossed the boundaries of making sex a part of our relationship. I was afraid of ruining it. The first tattoo I got was on my left knee: our initials inside of a heart.

I became a lot more unpleased with life. I drank more. Marijuana use became hard drug use—meth and speed. I was winding down, getting lost in a spiral of destruction. I hated myself and my life. I felt that things were just not fair for not having a normal life. I felt I wasn't accepted. I worried too much what others thought about me.

A dear friend of mine's mother once sat me down and told me, "I notice you are too worried about the acceptance of others. You care too much about what others think of you." It was then, I knew, she was onto something. She saw in me what I didn't recognize for myself.

I went all out and started with the feminine acting again, like when I was a young child. It bothered me when other people stared at me, and snickered about my character. I became angry toward others, especially when they didn't accept me for who I was. When I knew I was getting judged the anger really came with fury.

In and out of jail I went for fighting, and just being outright destructive. In my mind, the world revolved around me. I told myself, "If the world won't accept me, I will make them accept me."

In jail I had my first taste of what a transsexual was. I was in a pod where there were a lot of gays, transgendered, and individuals in protective custody. At first I was unsure about being friends with any of them. It was weird and foreign. But then, I was drawn toward how they could pull it off—the voice, the feminine characteristics, the whole gist of being a woman. I saw the attention that the men there in jail gave to these beautiful creatures. I began learning that all of them had things in common with me. We were all messed up from the time we were young, with not being accepted by family and society.

Many, if not all, had prostituted and been active drug users as well as alcohol lovers. I saw how each of these people had their own share of depression. They all had dreams and goals, but something was missing from these awesome people. At first, I wasn't sure what it was, but it finally came to me. These women had no ambition. No drive when it came to making all their dreams come true. Sure they talked about it, but I had never really seen any of them *being* about it.

I knew I was the same as them, but yet, so different. I slowly began blooming from the inside out, and I transformed into such a beautiful flower. My inside began to match the outside, and the dark cloud above, set to burst with storms, lifted and was gone. I knew what it felt like to care about myself. I knew what it felt like to say, "I love you," to me, and actually believe it.

My transformation was not done, I had to endure more growth. The light within me didn't begin to shine bright until I hit my rock bottom. I became homeless, prostituting for my next meal, my next hit, a place to shower and rest. I needed love. I needed to be validated by someone or something. I needed someone to slap me to my senses and tell me that they loved me and that they cared about what happened to me. Through karma, my violence finally handed me a prison sentence. I can clearly remember the judge telling me, "I don't feel comfortable releasing you back into society, for you are a menace to society." I felt offended by those words—deep inside, I had a hard time seeing myself as everyone else saw me.

Right before prison I was prostituting because I had an awful addiction to crack cocaine. I was trying to keep the man I was with and by keeping the crack cocaine coming nonstop, I for sure had him eating from the palm of my hand. He was a gentle giant, a great keyboard player with an incredible voice. If it weren't for the crack addiction I am pretty sure he would be all his music would allow him to be. He could sit in front of that keyboard and play a melody and belt out what was held inside him, and the tears would come. He had a gift. I knew that from the time we became acquainted with each other seven years before my incarceration.

I went by the name Jolene. He would always say, "Old Jolene here is crazy. You keep it up, you will end up prison." Sure enough, the day finally came. I was sent to prison for stabbing a guy in a jealous rage. All I could hear in my mind was my musician saying, "Didn't I tell you?"

This was my doorway. My doorway to manifesting my true desires. I had to go through everything I went through to become what I have become.

I was this pretty-looking thing with long hair, nails, and feminine characteristics sent away to a prison full of hard criminal-minded men. All I could think of is the bad things you hear about prison—about inmates raping other inmates, those who take advantage of the weaker ones, the notorious gangs and violence, and how the hell was I supposed to survive this?

In prison, I saw the worst of the worst. I met individuals who had no remorse for the crimes they had committed, who didn't really care that they would spend their last dying days confined to a penitentiary playground. I saw inmates get out on parole, and come right back in. The seed was planted that I would not be like that. I would get out, go home, and make something of myself. I knew I was gifted, and I knew I had the smarts to make it happen.

In prison I minded my own business. I stuck to a small group of people—those who have no problem being acquainted with someone like me. But it was tricky at times. Men would want to befriend me but for the wrong reasons. There were so many sharks in there. I engaged in relationships to aid my survival rate. I was told, "Don't get involved with someone who is looking at a lot of time, they will fall in love, and then, won't let you leave."

During that time I was interacting with a man that I had met in county jail. His final sentencing gave him a total of 64 years to life. I was devastated for I knew deep inside that our souls were mated. Through this experience and many others, I began to accept that life is not always fair, and that we don't always get the things we want, when we want them. And I believe, when this happens, it is a confirmation that God is not done with shaping us.

I survived all these hardships in life. I made it. Instead of going around it, I went through it. It made me a stronger person than I was before.

My release from prison was a day I will remember for as long as I live. Hearing the jail cells open to let me out for the last time was memorable. They opened. I walked out. And then, they closed.

I came back home to live with my family on the Wind River Reservation in Wyoming. I knew I had more work to do toward becoming my all. I had to work on successfully completing parole. I had to work on continued sobriety. I had to work on creating happiness within myself and shoot toward becoming all that I have been destined to be within my transition toward womanhood.

I have always wanted to become a best-selling author, become a productive member of society and do great things toward helping my community. Over five years, and with speaking everything into existence, I can now say, "I have accomplished all my goals."

I now have two books published: *It Never Happened* and *It Always Happens*. I am currently working on my third book, *It's Forever Happening*. I work hard for everything I'm blessed with in life. I make it a point to tell my hardship stories to those who will listen in hope that something I say will help in their lives—maybe someone who has struggled with making wrong decisions while under the influence of drugs and alcohol can benefit from my words. I am a true believer that everything happens for a reason and the light at the end of the tunnel shows itself lighter and brighter when we can begin understanding ourselves more.

I know that my journey is guided by something other than myself. I have grown a deep connection with what I call *The Creator*. To some it is God, Allah, Jehovah, the Universe, or the Divine. It is all the same. All religions preach and teach love. What matters is that the best intentions are in my mind, my conscience is clear, and that I have a good heart. Honesty is a must. I always speak well of others and work toward uplifting those who need an extra push.

Once feeling we are all familiar with in so many ways, is love. Love is the number one thing that saves people from themselves and from destruction. It starts with loving ourselves first. An ex once told me years ago, "How can you love me, when you don't even love yourself!" Those words have stuck with me, and I am so grateful for my ex choosing to share that simple message. It is a message that I took within my heart. I nurtured it and it grew—for the love I have for others now radiates from the love I hold deep in my heart for myself.

I am proud to say, I love me!

Darrah J. Perez is from the Wind River Indian Reservation in Central Wyoming. She writes stories and poetry in honor of her tribal ancestry and spirituality. Darrah is an enrolled member of the Blackfeet Nation in Browning, MT, but has blood roots in both the Northern Arapaho and Eastern Shoshone tribes of Wyoming. She supports efforts in all communities toward drug and alcohol recovery and supports mentorship programs involving all two-spirited individuals. Contact her at darrah.perez@gmail.com.

Hi, My Name's Alexis

Alexis Ivy

and I'm an addict and the more rain pours,
the more I remember I wasn't made for simple,
never learned anything simple. I wanted unadored,
left out, missed-out, to be unsayable,
a speech impediment. I love trouble,
know only trouble, licking the soles of any friend's
shoes, bark up the wrong lumber, the valid bullshit, the going-nowheres, the too many men,
the always-till-forevers, the habitually-bad-
beats. A dance with death to have a revelation,
to get back to fair shake, to water and mend. Had
to quit quitting on me to find salvation.
Bless being careful. Bless being mine
again, beautiful for the first last time.

Alexis Ivy's most recent poems have appeared in Sp*are Change News, The Santa Fe Literary Review, Eclipse, Yellow Medicine Review, Borderlands: Texas Poetry Review, J Journal*, and *The Worcester Review*. Her first poetry collection, *Romance with Small-Time Crooks*, was published in 2013 by BlazeVoX [books]. Alexis works at a homeless shelter and lives in her hometown of Boston. She has been clean since 2008 and is in NA.

The Turn I Took

Lucas Zulu

I was sick and tired of drowning in a glass
Monday to Sunday No Holiday

I could not afford to be trashed by you
Anymore while you squandered my precious time

I clung to you for many moons
At long last I unravelled the ribbon of our ties

I cut off the feet that hurried to your oasis
They led me to a fine mess

I realized that to bubble with excitement I could not lean on you
Happiness comes in different ways when I'm sober

I made a silent vow not to return to you
And today I sail through life without holding you in my hand

I cleaved to my choice even though it has never been easy
Nine years have passed without touching you

I no longer desire to immerse myself in your bottles
And now I cherish the turn I took when we parted at the crossroad

Lucas Zulu was born in South Africa and lives in Kwa-Guqa, Emalahleni, Mpumalanga province. His poems have appeared in *New Coin*, *Carapace*, *Stanzas*, *Africa! My Africa!*, *Africa Ablaze!*, *Heart of Africa!* and most recently in *The Best "New" African Poets 2015*.

MANY PATHWAYS

Introduction to Many Pathways

The New Recovery Advocacy Movement honors all pathways to recovery. As stated on the website of the organization, Faces and Voices of Recovery, "There are many (religious, spiritual, secular) pathways to recovery, and ALL are cause for celebration."

The stories and poems in this section highlight the diversity of ways that people find their way out of addiction. In the following pages, many a grateful nod is given to treatment and twelve-step programs. There is no argument: these are programs that save lives.

But recovery might also be a solo project, like the one Olive undertakes in "Salivate" by Caralyn Davis.

Or it could be an epiphany-provoked abstinence, as in "Last Call in Aberdeen: 1986" by John E. Simonds.

Or it might be a stumble onto the Red Road, like the one our poet Antonio Sanchez-Day took with the help of his good friend in "Taking On Life."

A spiritual undercurrent runs through this section, as when Pushcart Prize–winning poet Paul Hostovsky muses about the heroin addicts of Lynn, Massachusetts, who "find the idea of spiritual healing irreducible and beautiful."

The stories and poems that follow celebrate these many pathways and remind us not to judge people who use methods different from our own.

Taking On Life

Antonio Sanchez-Day

Ahau Bro,
I heard the news of you walking on the
other day. I will admit my heart sank at first
receiving the news, shock thundered in my spirit
as the raindrops of sadness fell. I unfortunately
cannot put tobacco down, or burned cedar, while
speaking to you right now, but I will when I get
to where I am going, I promise. I again was
disheartened by the news, but will not dwell in
sadness because I know you would tell me,
Aye! Knock it off! Behave! Instead I
will spend this moment in time talking
about how I knew you and how you affected
my life, and influenced me.

You are a friend, teacher, artist and
a warrior. We first met inside that place
behind them walls and razor wire, you remember?
We would walk endless miles round that
track talking 'bout our life's journey down that
black road that led us to that place. We
would exercise together getting our bodies
healthy again, I remember you always
shadow boxin', always trying to catch me

off guard with a jab or hook, eh, old man?
When it was lockdown you always sent
me back to my cell with things to ponder,
or them damn riddles which you would let
fester in my brain for days.

As time passed I finally came to you and
asked you to teach me about them doings.
You accepted my offering and proceeded to
fill my cup, quenching my thirst for knowledge
of the unknown. We would attend call-out
and go to our little section of land designated
to us in that place (the mini rez, eh?) and
sit around that fire. I was spiritually free,
you the teacher, I the student. Remember
how nervous I was handling the Chanupa
for the first time? Or how you would make
me sing traditional songs on call?
I reminisce on your stories of your personal
experience of the Sundance ceremony and
its beauty and healing power. I'd close my
eyes, listen and escape those walls and
envision your stories.

You taught me that warrior's path,
that a warrior looks at life as if he's going
into battle, taking on life. We did just
that. I recall all the times we fasted,
sacrificed, suffered, and prayed together
in that lodge. I call to mind times of war
where we literally stood back to back, blades
in hand defending what we believed in.
We shed blood, sweat, and tears together
'til we made it out of that place.

Our battles continued beyond those walls,
we fought the number one enemy, ourselves.
Yes, we both became fallen warriors to our
addiction, but upon hearing the news of you
walking on, I heard it was the Red Road
of sobriety you left this earth on. I am
going back to that place, to pay my dues but
am back on that warrior's path you taught
me. Until next time, my friend, when our paths
hopefully cross on that Red Road . . . I'll picture
you at the Sundance, attached to that tree
pierced through the chest with bone, blowing
your whistle to the sky, taking on life!

Anthony Sanchez-Day (Antonio), currently of Topeka, Kansas, is a 41-year-old Mexican/Native American male who has spent most of his life, since being a juvenile, in the cycle of addiction, and in correctional facilities. "Taking On Life" was written after Antonio learned of the passing of a friend who was very spiritual and influential in Antonio's recovery. His passing motivates Antonio in his pursuit of sobriety and spirituality.

Antonio reached three years of sobriety on April 23, 2016. He is living in an Oxford house and was just voted in as president. He advocates for the Oxford house as well as the pre-release program he participated in while incarcerated in El Dorado Correctional Facility. People who have been fundamental to Antonio's recovery include John Agnew, his recovery coach; Rob Ackerman, his mentor/sponsor; and Professor Daldorph, whose writing class in the Douglas County Jail helped Antonio to discover his talent as a writer. He also gives credit to Aurora, the Oxford house dog, who loves Antonio unconditionally.

Antonio plans to go back to school to earn his associate's degree so that he can enter the social services field. He wants to become a recovery coach and mentor and work with other addicts, ex convicts, and at-risk youth.

The Pigeons of Lynn

Paul Hostovsky

The pigeons of Lynn
are befouling the roof
of the Lynn Historical Society
on Green Street,
which from 1875 to 1882
was the home of Mary Baker Eddy
who moved around a lot
because her neighbors, the good
people of Lynn, Massachusetts,
were made to feel uncomfortable by
her original healings
which were spiritual in nature
and gave them the heebie-jeebies.

The pigeons of Lynn
are not spiritual in nature,
though here and there a sick or injured one
crouching on the sidewalk—
a little feathered stomachache
breathing among the footfalls—
could surely use one or two of Mrs. Eddy's
original healings.

And the recovering heroin addicts of Lynn
are trying to empty their minds of all but grace
under the roof of the halfway house
which from 1995 to the present day
has occupied the same mucous-green building
across from the Historical Society
on Green Street,
in spite of the fact that the neighbors, the same
good people of Lynn,
are made to feel uncomfortable by
the thought of a houseful of heroin addicts
living next door.

The heroin addicts of Lynn
may or may not have read the works of Mrs. Eddy,
though some have visited the Historical Society,
fingered an antique table, considered
asking the attractive docent
about morphine in New England in the 1880s.

Each night the pigeons quit
the roof of the Historical Society
for the roof of the halfway house
just after the sun goes down
behind the generous hundred-year oak.

The addict doesn't quit, say the staff
at the halfway house,
many of whom are recovering addicts
themselves. He changes
from the inside out. It's an inside job.
And even if they never
read any of the works of Mrs. Eddy
who was not a heroin addict
or a dove fancier

or a resident of Lynn
for long,
they find
the idea of spiritual healing
irreducible
and beautiful. It is, you'll hear them say
in their meetings on the top floor
just beneath the cooing ceiling joists,
quite simply the most important fact
of their lives.

Salivate

Caralyn Davis

Sunday: Day 1/Week 1

I drink every day, have for years. At the age of 29, it's my one committed activity. Wine is my thing, or gin and tonic if I go to a nightclub. I can't just stop. I try to picture myself: one day with alcohol, the next without it forever. The image won't coalesce. I can't afford rehab, and Alcoholics Anonymous smacks of group activities, which are beyond me since the great Girl Scouts debacle of my youth. My options are (1) revel Mardi Gras–style or (2) create a strategy using my own brand of steps to plod toward an alcohol-free existence.

I'm starting today. Sunday is the nominal day of rest, so I'm going to stop drinking on Sundays. When I feel okay with that, I'll add in Mondays, then Tuesdays, and so on and so forth until I'm clear seven days a week, 52 weeks a year. Doing Monday next will give me forward momentum. A white lie. I can't face Friday and Saturday. Christ, I hyperventilate at the thought of a weekend without alcohol. The corked maw of sobriety is frightening enough. I'll begin with the easiest days and work my way up.

The rationale behind my plan is this: I have a modicum of control, a base to build from. I'm a functional alcoholic, according to the alcoholism literature, because I don't drink 24 hours a day and I manage to hold down a semi-paying job.

I'm an Editor, after a fashion. The grandiosity of that full-throated capital "E" eludes me. True Editors corral the wayward meanderings of the next Thomas Wolfe. I edit television listings. In fact, I'm one of the few people on the planet who can spell the names, complete with proper hyphenation, of the perky stars of the Saturday morning teen comedy *Saved by the Bell*—Mark-Paul Gosselaar and Tiffani-Amber Thiessen. I could continue. But who the hell cares now, let alone in 50 years? I've been stuck in this lame-ass job for eight years, my annual salary skyrocketing from $13,500 to a plush $17,737.32 as a result of my eagle eye for inane editorial minutiae.

I started drinking to talk to people. It worked to a point, then diminishing returns. My friends from college have professional careers, fiancés, lives that don't include me. I don't even have a boyfriend. A trip to the grocery store breeds more than enough mental anguish. The thought of dating again makes my skin crawl.

Basically, I'm a borderline hermit in terms of human interactions. I get an occasional "Do you ever smile?" from the guy in the cubicle next to me at work. How am I supposed to answer a question like that? Make a joke? I don't know any, and he's not smiling when he asks so I don't think he's oozing friendliness himself. Tell the truth? "Well, Mark, if you could stop confusing ingenuous and ingenious in your local program descriptions or better yet stop using words like that altogether because viewers in the Dallas–Fort Worth area probably don't keep a dictionary handy when reading their TV schedules, then my life might be a tad more smile-worthy?" Too harsh. Instead I say, "Yes, I smile," and stare at him until he breaks eye contact.

So most of my conversations are limited to phone calls with Daddy. Poor man, he's willing to listen, and I need to vent. Freaking me out is not difficult. One question from my boss can send me into a tailspin.

"Will you have those listings for the San Francisco market done by noon?" she might say.

That's my cue to start obsessing: Did I miss the deadline? Is she mad at me? What did I do wrong? Is she going to fire me? She wants to fire me. I'm such an idiot. Stupid. So stupid. Is she going to fire me? These worries circle through my brain for days.

Some of it's a victimization complex, but to be fair to myself, strange, undeserved traumas occur with alarming frequency, like the time I got jumped by skinhead girls in a club parking lot. I promise, I don't wander around inciting violence in girls with mohawks and nose rings.

Last night I went out. I like dancing in a crowd where no one can tell who's alone. Of course, I drank. New twist: I had sex with a total stranger. I have a vague memory of meeting a guy. Don't remember the sex. The used condom was in the bathroom trashcan. As soon as I saw it, I vomited into the sink—I couldn't make the three extra steps to the toilet. My stomach kept convulsing. I leaned there, my forehead on the faucet, retching yellow stomach acid and then dry heaving. Five boyfriends in my entire life and now God knows who. Ick. Yes, the language of a two-year-old sums up the situation with awesome brevity and candor.

I tell Daddy a lot. The alcohol and the somewhat smaller bombshell that I've turned into a complete slut are off limits. Certain boundaries in the father/daughter relationship shouldn't be crossed. But I have my plan. I've been thinking about it for a few months. Truthfully, the verb upgraded to "pondering" when I passed the one-week mark on my thought processes. However, I needed that time. The road to alcoholism is paved with whims. Stopping requires determined thought and action.

I will do this. Reveling isn't my strong suit.

Monday: Day 2/Week 3
Thank God I decided to stop drinking during baseball season. I'm too nervous to read, I can't afford cable, and my little black and white TV gets one fuzz-free channel: TBS, the broadcast home of the Atlanta Braves. Go Braves!

I made it two Sundays in a row. Time to add a new day. So I've been sitting here in my studio apartment whiling away a Monday night, attempting to endure 48 consecutive hours without alcohol. The ballgame occupied a blissful three hours and 12 minutes of my evening. I'm aware of how pathetic that sounds.

Daddy called after the news, and we talked about the game. We started bridging the distance of my teen-age years right before I left for college. My classmates were excited. I sat on my bedroom floor, legs crossed, rocking myself and crying. Month after month. A lot of nights, Daddy came in and sat on the floor with me. "You'll get through this," he said. A sweet lie.

Don't get me wrong. I was mighty pleased to leave behind the hell of Stephens County High School. Daddy got transferred to a mill in Toccoa, that's north Georgia, before my junior year. I was transplanted into a high school distinguished by a 25-foot-tall Indian chief mascot and a complementary red and black color scheme that drenched the walls, floors, lockers, and every other paint-permeable fixture in the building. Football-crazed lunatics, anyone?

Actually, I like pro and college football. I've followed the Atlanta Falcons and Georgia Tech since I was young. My brother never liked sports. I started watching with Daddy so he wouldn't be alone. We even drag Mama to Tech games when Daddy gets free tickets from a dye salesman who knows he went to school there.

High school football is different, spurning the casual fan. A closed ecosystem, high school is awash in all things spirit-y, with the spirit ribbons you have to buy each week (or risk looking spiritless) and the mandatory-attendance pep rallies, where the principal leads the cheers and berates the unpopular students who are sitting in their own unpopular student section of the bleachers. Nothing quite like a 50-year-old authority figure screaming into a microphone at teenagers already in survival mode: "What's wrong with you people? You should be ashamed. Show some spirit!"

Half of us ignored him. The rest mumbled, "Go, Indians," whereupon a section filled with popular kids roared the gym down to put us in our place.

Anyway, first day in this spirit-mad high school, I showed up—with a transcript full of straight A's—in a blue plaid circle skirt, a white t-shirt, a three-strand necklace of bright blue plastic gumball beads from the 1950s, and the name Olive instead of Ashley or Savannah. Shy too. I might have been considered artistic somewhere else. Mired among the jeans-wearing, yee-hawing Stephens County Indians, I was a complete freak. The one thing that could have saved me from social disaster was unearthly beauty. I was a basic brown-haired teenager.

Junior year wasn't bad because Katie, a girl from New York, transferred in, and we were inseparable. Then she transferred back out. Senior year, my circle of friends was a triangle: me, a 90-pound guy in overalls who every other word emitted, "Hmmmmmmm," at a volume that made your skull vibrate, and a 300-pound girl who'd suffered brain damage as a child and was reading at a fourth-grade level. We were friends in the way of people who have nothing in common except loneliness. Talking to them kept me from imploding under the isolation. I wasn't the friend they wanted, the go to the movies and drink milkshakes at McDonald's and hang out at the lake friend, but at least I listened. No one else did.

Tuesday: Day 3/Week 5

Sunday, Monday, Tuesday. Three days a week free from alcohol. I don't want to consume extra on drinking days to compensate for the alcohol-free days so I'm using a measuring cup to pour the wine. I feel like a heroin addict being doled out methadone to survive detox. Still, I'm in charge of the doling and no cheating yet.

I'm rocking again, but I've got an actual rocking chair this time around. When Granny had to move into the nursing home before she died, she asked her children and grandchildren to come to her house and pick out keepsakes. I didn't go. Vulture feelings. My parents thought I'd regret it, so Mama and Daddy got me a set of china and a Bentwood rocking chair. I'm glad for the chair. I sit and rock and watch the Braves.

I also think about how I got in this mess. Back when I graduated from high school and was doing the first round of the aforementioned rocking and crying, Mama convinced Daddy I needed professional help. High school was a quantifiable, endurable hell. Safe. The unknowns of college floored me, in a literal sense. My parents responded to the crisis by taking me to a psychiatrist in Gainesville.

Nardil was the initial drug of choice. Consuming cheese can cause a person on Nardil to stroke out, so much of my first quarter at the University of Georgia was taken up with visions of my impending death. Then Ed, the sweaty psychiatrist who was less than a verbal gymnast himself, switched me to a new drug, Prozac.

I got thin and started smiling. That was enough to make Ed happy with my progress. He sent me back to UGA, a thin, smiling mute prepared with few social skills to make friends or date. I managed to stumble into Serena, Terri, and Susan thanks to dorm-enforced proximity, and they guided me through college with the help of some alcohol to combat the muteness. Not the best idea when I was on Prozac, but at the time it was kind of experimental and didn't come with the warning labels. Or none that I noticed.

We graduated and went to different cities, except Serena came to Atlanta with me when she got a job at Zoo Atlanta. I couldn't be on Daddy's insurance anymore. The visits to Ed stopped, the prescriptions too. Eventually I found my current dead-end job. Without any alcohol-infused chattiness, I had trouble talking during interviews, ergo the pickings were slim.

Petty concerns fed on Alice in Wonderland eat-me cake, smacking my brain against life's ceilings: "I express interest in people, ask questions— why do I get monosyllables and Serena gets a new friend every weekend? I can't afford an oil change. My car's going to break. Watch the dash, watch the dash. What'll I do if the light comes on? No boyfriend. Soon Mama's going to stop saying, 'Of course, you'll get married.' I'll die when she stops, when even she can't believe it. I'll die if she doesn't stop. No, I really don't think looking at silver patterns will be fun this weekend. That pain in my side must be a tumor. Broccoli prevents cancer. I've got to eat broccoli. Cheese is the Devil's food. Eat the damn broccoli, Olive."

I went to my new primary care physician and told her my former psychiatrist had prescribed Prozac. She gave me a prescription for the "standard dose" of 10 milligrams. It was like swallowing an M&M whole—no crunchy candy shell, no creamy chocolate goodness, no pleasing round conduit of happiness. I was frantic. I dug up one of my old prescription bottles, and that's when I discovered I'd been a lab rat. My daily dose from Ed: 120 milligrams.

The new doctor stared at me.

"There's no way I can prescribe that," she said. "You'd have to see a psychiatrist, and I don't think they'd go over eighty milligrams a day."

My health plan didn't cover psychiatric visits. I went full-time on the alcohol.

Wednesday: Day 4/Week 8

I've discovered carbonated water. It's a gift from God. The lost Jewish people stumbling around the desert got manna, I get bubbly water. Perrier's my favorite, but the budget favors Crown. Its bubbles are harsh, man-made. They bombard your lips and tongue. On the bright side, the assault takes your mind off the lack of alcohol in your mouth. I'm drinking about four bottles a night.

My apartment is located across the street from a bar and a liquor store that share a parking lot. The owner of the liquor store gives me a bright smile when I come in at night and buy water instead of wine. He seems proud of me.

I've passed the halfway point. Four days out of seven not drinking. Yeah me. The celebration is short-lived. Staying on schedule is getting harder. I plot out what minute of what day I can next have alcohol. I rock in my chair and count down the hours until I'm tired enough to pass out—usually around 3 a.m. I'll have to buy my water at Kroger on the way home from work. Going in the liquor store is no longer safe.

Thursday: Day 5/Week 12

Fuck, I say. And say and say. Which is odd, considering my sheltered self never used the word until I crossed paths with Serena during our freshman year at UGA. She was from New Jersey. Still is, but a year after we came to Atlanta, she gave me two days' warning and moved away to a new job and a new life in Arizona. I didn't think my best friend would do that. These days we don't talk. Back when we first met, she wore black leather and her hair was long, blond, and frizzy kind of like a female Ramone except hot and sexy instead of mostly creepy like an actual Ramone if you've ever seen one, and she said "Fuckin' A" 100 times a day.

I didn't understand what it meant, didn't like to ask. Our friends seemed to know already. When I was growing up, cursing wasn't an option. The worst I ever heard Daddy say was "Rats!" when he was steaming mad.

Same with Mama, almost. One summer when we were visiting Granny, Mama, Daddy, my brother Ted, and I went to the store to get something, maybe dried beef, which was a popular lunch item back when Ted and I ate meat. We hadn't gone half a mile before Mama took off her shoe, slammed it into the dashboard, and yelled, "Shit!"

No one said anything for a minute. Then I pulled myself together.

"What's wrong?" I said.

"Your grandmother can be a bitch sometimes." Mama's voice quavered on the word bitch. I'd never heard her say that either.

A little more quiet. Finally she said, "I'm sorry I got upset." The heel of the shoe had gouged a chunk of vinyl out of the dashboard. I put my arms around her shoulders from the backseat and kissed the side of her neck. Ted scooted over from his side and patted her head. Daddy started driving left-handed so he could hold her hand with his right. Later we teased her.

Fuck. I would very much like a drink, thank you. Please. Please. Fuck.

Friday: Day 6/Week 20

Here we go: Six days a week without alcohol. Moving past five days was a sticking point. I needed several weeks to acclimate to the idea of giving up Friday and Saturday. All right, it was two months, but I did keep Sunday through Thursday alcohol-free, and that's damn good. I've had help. Both Daddy and my cat can tell something's wrong. These days, Daddy talks to me for more than an hour a night—his phone bill must be astronomical. Marmalade stakes out a spot on my lap and lets me pet his head until bedtime. He doesn't mind the rocking. I think he's trying to keep my hands busy.

I went to see my old boyfriend Paul yesterday, to say hello. We'd stayed friends after we both moved on to new people. A bulbous half-empty jug of red was on the floor next to the sofa. Paul picked it up as we sat down. His finger hooked through the glass handle and set the jug swinging.

"Want some?" he said. We drank a lot in our time together. The wine sloshed from side to side in the jug. Heavy seas.

I said no. He poured himself a jelly glass. We met when I was dating a drummer. I'd thought that boyfriend was the love of my life. Of course, I hadn't experienced much in the way of love—or normal dating. He and I ended things quickly, but Paul stuck it out with me quite a while. He listened to my sad crap and found ways to cheer me up, as well as breaking into my apartment on a monthly basis to rummage through my underwear drawer. I couldn't hold it against him. We both had our insane moments. I almost kicked his door in once. (The lock was quite strong.)

Black hair, brown eyes, motorcycle. He was so fun, and dear God, he could fuck. The last time was when his then-latest girlfriend was out of town. We ended up in her apartment to watch a video of the David Lynch movie *Blue Velvet*. Neither of us could afford high-tech equipment like a VCR. We were watching the movie, drinking wine, and Paul put his hand on my leg. A simple sign of affection between friends, nothing new, but somehow it led to a hot, rough fuck right on the girlfriend's couch.

He felt bad. I knew I should too, yet I still considered him mine in a way, which was stupid and strange because he was not mine anymore and I didn't want him to be, not romantically. I just needed that connection.

Most of my boyfriends have said to my face, "You're strange, you know."

Thanks. That's the sort of Cinderella talk girls yearn to hear. Paul made me feel like I belonged. Now Paul goes to work, he comes home to his shitty apartment, he drinks, he writes. While I was there, he read me a chapter of the novel he's working on. A rambling mess. His genius is drowning, and he can't tell.

Saturday: Day 7/Week 23

There's a park about two miles from my apartment. I walk down there and back every day. I take my Walkman and listen to the Ramones/Sex Pistols mix tape my brother Ted made me when I was struggling to survive the three-mile runs in my Fitness for Life class in college. I feel better when I'm done. Then I rock and watch the Braves. I can read some, Harlequin Romances not Proust, but it's a start. Daddy and Marmalade remain vigilant.

During this whole weaning process, I've had trouble taking out the trash. I'm not sure why. I bag up the bottles and leave the bags stacked on the screen porch instead of taking them to the dumpster.

I do know why—partly. I'm ashamed of the bottles. That's nothing new. However, it's worse. I've been hoarding them over the last six months. Like one of those old people you see on the news: The 89-year-old woman dies, and when the police force the door of her home, they find newspapers going back to 1912 stacked to the ceiling in each room. Or the 70-year-old man who's squirreled away 150,000 tin cans has a heart attack, and the ambulance crew has to navigate the house inching through tiny vegetable- and chili-lined footpaths. Except my apartment would be lined with empty wine bottles.

Last night I think I had a dream that something was crawling on my neck. I reached up and grabbed it and threw it across the room. I heard it thump. This morning I checked to see if a dead mouse or rat body was splayed against the wall. Nothing. It still felt more like a memory than a dream. I took out the trash. I walked down to the dumpster in the parking lot. Seven trips. Fifteen bags. They all clinked.

I scrubbed down the apartment when I was done. Mid-afternoon, Kroger. I loaded mousetraps and an early edition of the Sunday paper into the cart so that, respectively, I could stalk stray rodents and look over the classifieds. I wanted the perfect Sunday morning breakfast morsel. Pondering the merits of Lucky Charms vs. Eggo waffles, my concentration lapsed and I cruised the aisles on autopilot.

I froze when I realized where I was. I'd turned down the aisle to my old stomping grounds, and I was trapped, adrift in a gleaming river of coaxing libations. My eyes focused on a 1.5 liter Zinfandel. Dark, plummy undertones beckoned below a layer of green glass. My mouth filled with saliva, pooling under my tongue like I was one of Pavlov's dogs.

I swallowed and spun the cart around with military precision. Then I ran. I ran, and I speed-walked through the store in alternating bursts. Most people averted their gaze as I passed. The running, the tears, the speed-walking, the tears, the running. Take your pick. Any of it could have put their city-dwelling isolationist instincts on alert. But halfway down the soup and pasta aisle, a 60ish lady in an ankle-length red velour robe and leopard-print heels stared at me in disgust. Like I was some shameful oddity. Like there wasn't plenty of crazy to choose from on that aisle. I kept going, a study in rolling commotion.

I slowed to a pure walk as I reached a checkout lane.

The clerk and the security guard had been watching my approach and stood side by side. "You in a hurry?" the guard said. "You can't run in here, makin' trouble."

I wiped my cheeks with one hand and began unloading the cart with the other.

"I'm good." I flashed him a smile. "No more trouble."

This story was originally published in The Great Smokies Review, *a publication of the Great Smokies Writing Program and the University of North Carolina–Asheville.*

Caralyn Davis lives in Asheville and works as a freelance writer for trade publications in the healthcare and technology transfer fields. Her fiction and creative nonfiction have appeared in *Word Riot, The Doctor T. J. Eckleburg Review, Superstition Review, Monkeybicycle, Eclectica,* and other journals. Her faves include homemade orange marmalade and grouchy gray cats. "Salivate" is about building yourself into who you want to be—creating conditions for small successes that can enable you to reach your goals of health and well-being—no matter how difficult and frightening the prospect.

Raven

David Olsen

My erstwhile best friend
and latter-day worst enemy waits.
To him I've surrendered more

than most people ever possess.
My travelling companion
to wherever I call home

is nominally 12 years old
but, unopened, has matured
to 13 . . . 14 . . . 14½.

An ever-accusing presence
on dresser, desk or shelf,
the raven is vigilant, challenging.

A glass, poor Yorick?
Old Crow's little joke.
Go to hell. I can be brave

in the afternoon's test of will
when I forget that I still
have to make it through the night.

NB: Old Crow is a Kentucky bourbon whiskey.

Reprinted from Unfolding Origami *(Cinnamon Press, © 2015 David Olsen);* Sailing to Atlantis *(Finishing Line Press, © 2013 David Olsen); and* The Babel Anthology #1 *(© 2012 David Olsen).*

David Olsen's *Unfolding Origami* won the Cinnamon Press Poetry Collection Award. His three poetry chapbooks are from US publishers. His work appears in anthologies and journals on both sides of the Atlantic. Formerly an energy economist, management consultant, and performing arts critic, he now lives in Oxford, England. "Raven" depicts his impressions of how some reformed addicts, whatever their particular weakness, challenge or dare themselves with temptation. Each day is a test, which may or may not be successfully passed.

Our Better Angels

Maureen Geraghty

My father was never mean to my siblings and me when he was drunk. He prided himself on being a good dad, playing the part by day, going to work, cutting the grass, and playing Monopoly on the living room floor with us when he got home. His can of Tab was laced with vermouth, his cans of Pabst Blue Ribbon stacked up the garbage. As the evening went on, his cheery dad act got sloppy and his eyes blurred with a rage only aimed at our mother. After my father quit lawn work and family games, he and my mother sat at the kitchen table and argued while my brother, sister, and I got our pajamas on and played. The nights were patterned in routine.

Being the oldest, I was on to my dad. Secretly, I watched the nightly fights like a spectator at a sports arena. I was curious and protective. Was this the same man I adored, swearing at my mother, accusing her of ridiculous things while he pounded his fist, slurring his angry words? My siblings and I saw every ugly act, heard every hideous exchange, felt their tension so tightly through their plastered smiles and "let's pretend nothing happened" mornings of pancakes and bacon.

After a night of boozy brawls and promises of never-agains, my brother would stand on a stool and show us bottles hidden in the ceiling panes or walk us out to the garage and point to buckets and bins that stored liters of vodka. He knew. The youngest knew just as much as the middle and the oldest child. We lived in a home built of four alcoholic walls. The place of shames prettied over and ignored and Jekyll and Hyde anxieties of wondering who will be there when you walk through the door. The never-have-any-friends-over house because the risk of humiliation was too great and the lies, too exhausting. We all grew around our father's illness like sprouts that grow off a fallen nurse log, tangled and awkward but trying to keep something alive.

Flash forward. I am an adult. Successful job, a beautiful son and daughter, and a marriage that didn't work out. I am like my father and become a teacher. I work with the hardest kids with the hardest lives. They confide in me stories about their strung-out moms, incarcerated fathers, holidays drowned and doped.

I want to save every one of them. But when I get home, I pour another glass of wine because those edges forever need taking off and I can't deal with my own pain much less the pain my students feel. I, too, have become master of smoke and mirrors. Only let others see what I think they want to see and meanwhile I'm an echoing shell of a woman. A desperate, lonely woman whose happy hours are filled with sad.

I don't think I have a problem. I have lots of problems but not *that* problem. I live on in my charade. Peace is just a gulp away. But then there is the guilt, the 3:00 a.m. demons who scream in my dreams, "You are a bad person!" So I promise I won't have as much or won't drink alone, on an empty stomach . . . I promise, make deals with God, vow to never again—and I see my brother's innocence in my own son's face. Deep down I know my own daughter sees I'm not good-mommy when I fall asleep during story time, not quite present, not okay until I've uncorked and swallowed. I have become my father. The "let's pretend" days enter my adult home. And though I swore I would never be that way, here I am—all bargains, regret, guilt, fake, and fear. Oh, and the fear is a chisel that chips at me until I feel stressed and stiff, the kind of stiff a drink could fix. Outside, I keep the appearance of fine. Inside, I am just numb, afraid and far from fine.

One night I have wine before trick-or-treating, the night before my daughter's eighth birthday. I walk the dark and decorated streets with my kids. We pass porches of jack-o-lanterns, goblins, and stringy spider webs. They lug orange pillowcases and gather Almond Joys, Kit Kats, and M&Ms. The parents bring flasks of Merlot and are offered adult treats of beer and flavored liquor.

The next morning, I remember nothing of how we got home. Halloween is a patchwork of blur. My daughter walks in my room wearing her new birthday pajamas and I have no idea when or how she got them. Black out. Black. Out. A chunk of life erased from my memory. I freeze in absolute panic.

Something bigger than me picks up the phone to call a friend. Something bigger than me says, "You will not miss your life. You will not mess up your kids. You *will* break this cycle. You are done with alcohol." Done. Wait, never? I could not conceive of that never. But the angels on the other side of the phone swept me up. I didn't have to think of never or ever or tomorrow. I promised I would meet a woman I barely knew at a church basement near my house. Something bigger than me said, "Just go." My daughter in her new pajamas. Her face so excited for a birthday. My face, hiding my remorse and terror. Something bigger than me said, "It's not about you anymore. Surrender for them."

I got myself to the church, nervous and trembling from both alcohol and lack of it. The angels surrounded me, brought me coffee, and had me sit next to them. As the hum of the twelve steps and the preamble swirled around my head, I looked around at the large crowd. I had never seen such a diverse group of humans in the same room—young, old, some with scruffy beards and others in suits. Women and teen boys. Black, brown, and white.

I listened. I heard story after story of hope. Even the ones who confessed to the most humiliating situations sat in gratitude, proclaiming that without the final surrender, they would not have the peace and authentic support experienced in their lives today.

I kept coming back. I continued to drag my confused, scared, and lost self back to the metal chairs and the angels.

I keep going back. I pick up the phone and do what is suggested. Life is not easy, but it is not drunk.

Every time I doubt or don't want to go to a meeting, I think of the children. How I am breaking the cycle of addiction for them. Not only for my own kids, the daughter in her birthday pajamas and the son who shines my brother's face, but for all the kids I teach every day whose families also are housed between the angry, sad walls of alcoholism and drug addiction. God willing, I will have one year of continuous sobriety next week. I pray to be an angel, too.

Maureen Geraghty has taught in alternative high schools for over 25 years. She has published poems in mamazine.com, mothing.com, and *ReThinking Schools,* and self-published a book, *Look Up: Poems of a Life.* The National Writing Project featured her article "Writing Outside the Bars" in their journal, *The Quarterly.* Currently, she is co-authoring a book based on that article entitled *Between Writers and Lifers,* and maintains a Facebook page with the same name. Maureen is the proud mother of two school-age children. They live in Portland, Oregon.

Last Call in Aberdeen: 1986

John E. Simonds

I had to quit drinking because my good self and bad
woke together each morning and dueled.

They never dreamed of an April in Scotland.

They quarreled as though I weren't there—
or maybe because I was—bad me asking
if he had really sung that old college song,
led the merry-go-round chorus,
climbed on a table to lift the crescendo?
Backyard birds added tunes of their own,
chasers to go with the morning wrangle.
Good me, slashing at first, now quiet and nodding,
saying much with silence—a truce of sorts.
Well, people enjoyed your enjoyment, good self conceded.

Did I really say what you said I said? bad me asked.
Well, it's all right, your boss was laughing, good me assured.
I feel awful, bad me confessed.
It's okay. You'll get over it—so will everyone else,
good me couldn't resist a cheap thrust,
letting us know he wasn't *all* good.

Pre-dawn settlings grew longer—
bad self more sorry, good more sardonic in yielding,
me the guy in the middle, judging family quarrels
no fun the day after in bed,
best left to people sharing privacy's prize.
Stopping short of danger was easy;
arguing wasn't, both sides wanting
issues, not satisfaction.

They never saw Scotland coming.

Good self reassured us in teasing ways
that deepened the hook.
Impartial self needed reason for both sides to stop.
Enough with the old-school moments,
insulting punch lines, hazy joustings, stupid jibes,
all leaping from ponds of sarcasm—
bugs flying about, tempting to be caught—
a world of predators and prey
fed by seconds of laughter.

Mai-tai is your tai, my old times sang
in nasal Rudy Vallee improv,
and those brandy milkshakes
were what made Alexander great,
bad guy had exhorted, toasting
Golden Sunrise with Harvey Wallbanger
and all the other Gallianos,
together chasing salty dogs
around the rim of midnight Margaritas,
some tequila for our border friends
and quinine tonic as a booster shot
in case those pond bugs bit us overnight.

The Scottish solution surprised us,
ancestral awareness dawning
that even fun kept a watch on its bar code.

Now the wake-ups are shorter,
bird greetings a seraphim choir.
A surface tension of memories
has taken the bait of conscience
and calmed its way to reflection:

Three straight scotches for breakfast
at Aberdeen proved unlikely grounds
for stopping cold on a day that began
with screeching gulls and friendly fishermen
sharing their galley of North Sea success,
Try this at home and get hung out to dry
with a fall from the afternoon masthead:
good and bad me now on the same page,
a *genie* of cheer that seemed worth distilling,
a ship-log memory to improve with age,
a bottle of bonded joy still sealed
for another sun, another yardarm.

John E. Simonds, 80, a retired reporter and newspaper editor, has lived in Hawai'i for 40 years. A Bowdoin College graduate, he has been writing verse since the 1970s. John is the author of *Waves from a Time-Zoned Brain* (AuthorHouse, 2009) and *Footnotes to the Sun* (iUniverse, 2015) and has had poems published in *Connecticut River Review, Bamboo Ridge Press, Hawai'i Pacific Review, The Ledge*, and New Millennium Writings. Recently his work was accepted for publication by *The New Guard* and *St. Petersburg Review*.

John says,

I didn't start drinking until my 20s and gradually grew comfortable with "social drinking" at people's homes, after work in bars and restaurants, occasionally at lunch. Alcohol seemed a personality enhancer, encouraging my role as an impromptu entertainer at gatherings. After some years, though, I became uncomfortable with morning-after reconciliations with my sober self and my wife.

In my 40s I tried cutting back, lowering my intake, letting others perform, but much of the need remained. The trip to Scotland (age 50) in April 1986 coincided with unrelated but troubling career events, and the cold air of an Aberdeen waterfront made three breakfast scotches seem like smooth soft drinks that might go on tasting good forever. Drinking is never going to be any better than this, I thought in a bright mood, but I surprised myself by thinking deeper.

What if it does become better and leads to a never-ending quest to replicate this feeling? In Hawai'i I had friends who made midday and after-work bee-lines from our newsroom to the welcoming bar nearby, an occupational rite for too many. But none of us ever drank three scotches before 9 a.m.

Scotland, home of 19th century ancestors, awakened me to the great taste of morning scotch in a fishing boat galley and a signal I didn't expect. I stopped while the good flavor lasted and haven't had any since, not even beer or a birthday champagne. I'm not as much fun at parties, but I don't regret it.

Releasing the Elephants

Karina Muñiz

We don't talk about the elephants in our living room. They show up every weekday night after 5 p.m. On weekends they often arrive as soon as the clock strikes noon. But sometimes it's hard not to acknowledge them, and contrary to the notion that elephants have impeccable memories, these ones always forget.

I sneak around their big feet and long leathery tails, and pretend that their toenails aren't chipped and broken, and that their hide isn't dry and chafing. After all, they can still walk. When their eyes turn glossy and their trunk curls up, I brace myself for their wailing. I listen to what they do remember: their tales of missed opportunities, wrong turns, and the harsh words spoken about them. They have forgotten about their sacred presence at temples, and do not see the power they hold even in the eyes of their predators. They have been told to believe otherwise. That's what's been locked in their memories.

So they sit in our living room, eating too many peanuts, and overworking their organs. Our neighbors never see them. They are, despite their size, masters at being invisible. Only we, and a select few, know they are there.

Except that one time, when they came back bloodied and bruised. "Poachers," they said, attacked them in the middle of the night.

* * *

What does recovery look like for me as an Adult Child of Alcoholics? In trying to answer that question, I can feel the guilt and shame moving around in my tightened chest like loose phlegm. It's easier to write in metaphor; I still want to protect my parents. By admitting that I am an Adult Child, they are implicated.

I have had my own battles with addiction in high school, college, and throughout my twenties. I have slipped now and then since. When I woke up on those occasions without remembering what exactly happened, I was transported back to the mornings, when I was younger, when I felt the coldness of the bathroom tile on my face and forearm, the pounding in my head while I peeled myself off the floor. The toilet seat was still up as I looked in the mirror and saw bloodshot pupils, bags under my eyes, and a tile imprint on my cheek. I tried piecing together the shameful images from the night before, after alcohol had taken over my body.

I'm afraid of these mornings, and the times when I don't always have control. But I know doing the work and gaining control starts with looking back. I sat down in front of my altar the other day, and asked my ancestors to help me break this cycle. They know I have been doing some research on our lineage.

This ever-elusive work that must be done—I'm trying to sort out what exactly that means. It's inquisitive and vacillates between wanting to understand my parents' addiction, and allowing myself to feel all the emotions that come with growing up behind a veil of denial and excuses. How do I explain all the discordant feelings toward them that are locked away in my knotted back and stiff neck? I was never without. My parents taught me the value of education and equity, and love me deeply. And yet I struggle for what they couldn't give me: a sense of security and self-worth when I lost them to their nightly anesthetic.

After I was born my mother started a journal for me. My birth was its own miracle. I had a 50-50 chance of being born with Trisomy 13, and dying before the age of two. The doctor had recommended an abortion, but my parents went through with the pregnancy, choosing to love me whether I was with them for days, months, or years. My mother wrote to me in the journal when I was seven, "It is only because of you that I can begin to really believe in myself. My only problem when I was pregnant was I couldn't drink. I'm glad I had 'this problem.' If I had had this problem after your birth, I would have saved a lot of grief."

She wrote about the sadness of her childhood, the constant criticism from her mother, of the loss at an early age of the women in her family who had truly loved her, and how God was the only reprieve from her drinking and deep depression.

For the number of times my mother has tried to quit in earnest, she is like Sisyphus and my father the boulder that stops them from reaching the top of the hill. They have been on this mountain for over 40 years now. Drinking is so embedded in our culture and my father's generation that the only time it's discussed as a problem is when a crisis hits. And even then an excuse is found. When my father had a serious fall, he said he was pushed from behind. When his cousins died of liver cancer, at least they had enjoyed some pleasures in life before they went.

This past Christmas my parents were going to meet my partner's family for the first time. This doesn't always happen in queer relationships, and the journey toward acceptance by both sides has been a long one. There was much to celebrate.

My mother bought gifts for all my partner's nieces and nephews and made a genuine effort to get to know the family, pushing through her shyness that often inhibits her. Still, instead of relishing a moment I would never have thought possible several years ago, I found myself fixated on my mother's wine glass, and on how many shots of whiskey my father had requested from the couch as he watched football. If my mother coughed, I rushed to her side with a glass of water and a worried look. I overindulged on the coquito my partner's mother had prepared, watered down my parents' drinks, and devised a plan of action in my head should there be another fall or outburst.

Despite the success of the long-awaited connection between families, I still felt exhausted afterward, ready to crawl up in a fetal position under the covers for the next couple of days. I'm not sure which impacted me more: the drinking or the incessant criticism from my father as I drove six hours there and back with my partner and parents in the car. But this is how I generally feel after spending time with my family, and I wanted to understand. I downloaded the *Adult Children of Alcoholics (ACA) Fellowship Text* on my Kindle, and started to read.

One of the many characteristics of ACAs that hit home for me was our tendency to work grueling hours at the expense of health and social life, and usually it is fear of authority figures or people-pleasing traits in action.

I have never known how not to go hard. I went from being the lost, scapegoat child who started drinking at 12 years old to an overachiever by 18. I still managed to go to school and graduate, because in my family we all "functioned"—unlike my cousins who were locked up, or who had moved on to heroin.

I had enough middle-class privilege to go away to college, and when I got to Chicago to study, I found an additional way to channel my anger and addictive tendencies. I was in search of my identity as a mixed-race Mexican/Swedish kid, and drawn to social justice. Xenophobia was on the rise in California, my home state. Proposition 187 had recently passed, which denied public services to undocumented communities. Seeing what was unfolding I began to get involved in the immigrant rights movement. Earlier that year the North American Free Trade Agreement (NAFTA) passed, creating greater inequities between the US and Mexico, and forcing more people to migrate. On the eve of NAFTA's enactment, the Zapatista Army of National Liberation (EZLN) in Chiapas, Mexico, began their uprising against neoliberalism. They called for their right to dignity, land, and recognition as indigenous communities. Several years later, during my first internship, I petitioned the US Congress to support human rights observers as the Zapatista struggle and movement unfolded in southern Mexico.

Twenty-two years have passed since then. I am still an organizer, believing in a world based on racial, gender, and economic justice. I learned to scream and shout, and organize and strategize to dismantle a system I know in my heart is unjust. And while the work is powerful and bigger than all of us, it created fertile ground for me as an Adult Child to lose myself in the movement and never slow down.

Recently my body got tired of me ignoring its subtle pleas, and decided to crank it up a notch. The pain in my forearms, wrist, and back grew debilitating, and I was diagnosed with Repetitive Stress Injury (RSI). I was told I would get better if I stopped typing and overworking my forearms. I work full time at a Latina immigrant rights base-building organization, and I go to school at night for an MFA in creative writing. Stop typing? That wasn't an option.

My first reaction was to have a temper tantrum. *I'm never going to be a writer!* I sobbed to my partner. *I've finally gotten my writing schedule going, and now this!* And then fear kicked in. How am I supposed to do my job? They're going to fire me.

It's been just under a year since my diagnosis, and I have pulled myself out of the drama vortex. My RSI is manageable for now, and has taken me on a deeper journey. The addiction to grueling hours just can't happen anymore. So how do I stop? It starts with noticing the patterns— of how as an Adult Child I want to take care of everyone else first, constantly please others, and lock myself into self-deprecation that leaves me burned out and feeling shitty, despite my accomplishments.

For the last several years I have been working on a coming-of-age memoir about a young woman on the run, in search of herself, living in cities in and outside of the US just long enough to get restless. I am learning the craft, strengthening my prose. I am trying to keep my relentless perfectionism, and the nasty critic who tells me I can't write and have nothing important to say, out of my head. I've been writing drafts that focus on how this woman experiences race, gender identity, and being mixed-heritage. But there's one block that has been stopping me from telling the full story, and that's being honest about the addiction she grew up in. It's why she started running away in the first place.

They say coming out is a process that happens in different ways and times in one's life. That has certainly been the case for me, and this recovery feels like that too. I'm in another phase of coming out. I'm starting with this story, shaking off the shame about what happens to so many families behind closed doors. I am standing behind my little-girl self at five years old, whispering to her words of love and encouragement about who she will become one day as I brush and braid her hair. She is playing with her Transformers at the top of the stairs, making up stories about the triumph of Optimus Prime in the shadows of the television's glare, while she waits for the elephants to release her parents from their grip.

Karina Muñiz is a queer Xicana writer and Community Engagement Fellow at Mills College where she is working on her MFA in Prose. She facilitates creative writing workshops for immigrant and household worker leaders in Oakland and San Francisco and believes in the power of storytelling to heal and open hearts and minds. Karina is also a contributing writer for the *Race, Poverty and Environment (RP&E)* journal, and a contributing author in the book *Working for Justice: The LA Model of Organizing and Advocacy* (Cornell University Press). She holds master's degrees in Urban Planning and Latin American Studies from UCLA, and is an alumna of the Voices of our Nations Arts Foundation (VONA).

Anonymous Meets Mona Lisa on the Road to Recovery

Ron Watson

When we first met, you had to convince me
that Mona Lisa was your real name.
It took you a while.
But it began to make sense, sort of—
you, a house painter by trade; you, whose smile
I had previously admired from across these rooms.
Honestly, with an open mind
I should not have been surprised to find myself
conversing with Mona Lisa, painter.
Then, as we talked behind Her red doors
inside the parish hall of St. Mary's,
you complained that your brushwork on a ceiling
kept you looking up all day. *That's Michelangelo,*
I thought; now, I know she's just blowing smoke.
Since therapy, I have only three brain cells,
and they are fighting. The elders say anything
might be a hint from a Higher Power, so I watch
and listen a lot, which brings me to tonight
and what happened at our sobriety celebration.
Holy Mother of Jesus.
My sponsor never advised a course of action
should Mona Lisa wearing cowboy boots
approach and ask me to dance.

What page is that on in the Big Book?
I was praying for some kind of sign when the DJ
called it a night and turned the house lights up.
I have no idea what this might mean—the god
of my understanding speaks a lost language,
and I have enough trouble with English.
I can tell you this:
I came straight home and danced all by myself
three jigs. I wore my shadow out.
You should have seen me reel.

This poem originally appeared in Zone 3, *Volume XIII, no. 1.*

Ron Watson is an American poet, born in 1958 in Little Rock, Arkansas. He claims to have "turned to poetry instead of crime in 1976." In 1992, Ron received an Al Smith Fellowship for Poetry from the Kentucky Arts Council. His work has appeared in numerous publications including *Slant* and *Southern Poetry Review.* His chapbooks include *My Name Ain't Bud* (Pygmy Forest Press, 1991), *Pagan Faith* (Nightshade Press, 1992), *A Sacred Heart* (Redneck Press, 1994), and *Counting Down the Days* (Pudding House Press, 1994). Ron wrote this poem after it happened to him one night. He has been alcohol-free since November 14, 1995.

FAMILIES MATTER

Introduction to Families Matter

As family members and loved ones of people in or seeking long-term recovery, we have our own journeys. We suffer too, and may find that, like Chelsea Lai in "Get Your Ass to Al-Anon," we are "wasting precious time, stressing out, trying to control the uncontrollable."

Like Patricia McDaniel, in "Family, Interrupted," we fumble and fall. We get angry. Eventually we are forced to grasp the hard but essential truth: sometimes we are just too close to help.

We may, like A. Z. Roa in "Chile Roasting Season," have to leave our sick and addicted loved one in someone else's hands for a time.

We discover, like Kristina Cerise, in "Shall We Set a Place for Peggy?," that honesty is the best recovery policy and start "to live with messy and uncomfortable truths."

As we reach for our own brand of recovery, we grow and change. We learn that addiction is a brain disorder, not a moral failing. Most of all, we hold on to hope.

We keep trying and pray that our support for our loved ones will be a bridge to help them cross over to a new life in recovery, and not scaffolding that holds them in place in their addiction.

Sometimes it's hard to know.

Sometimes we get it wrong.

That's part of our recovery story too.

Family members have a great opportunity. We can join those in recovery in stepping away from stigma's shadow. We can tell our stories and become what William L. White calls "recovery carriers—people . . . who make recovery infectious to those around them by their openness about their recovery experiences, their quality of life and character, and the compassion for and service to people still suffering from alcohol and other drug problems."[1]

---

[1] William L. White, "Recovery Carriers" (2012), available at www.williamwhite papers.com and www.facesandvoicesofrecovery.org.

Should We Set a Place for Peggy?

Kristina Cerise

Years ago, we discovered it was easier to invite people to our house for Christmas dinner than to accept an invitation elsewhere. I enjoy preparing a formal dinner, my kids enjoy staying in pajamas until the last possible moment before guests arrive, and my husband enjoys better-than-average lunch leftovers in the week that follows.

I love cooking for a crowd and setting a fancy table. I love the timeless patterns of my china and the gleam of the dining room chandelier captured in crystal glasses placed *just so* above the knives with brushed silver handles. I love arranging the serving dishes to showcase the range of colors: vibrant butternut squash, crisp-tender green beans, and moist ham edged in the brown of a perfect glaze. I love the delicious irony of placing green Jell-O salad on a fancy platter and setting it alongside sophisticated recipes that feature tarragon or truffles.

This year, as I stand at the stove stirring the roux and deciding whether the forest green napkins embroidered with pinecones or the plain navy napkins are more striking against the subtle poinsettia embroidery on my ivory tablecloth, my husband interrupts my reverie.

"Should we set a place for Peggy?"

"What?"

"For Peggy. Are you going to set a place at the table for Peggy?"

I'm not sure how to read the look in his eyes. There is a heaviness; this isn't a casual question. In my peripheral vision I see my mother-in-law turn toward me, awaiting my answer.

"No. I wasn't planning on it. She's not coming. We all know she's not coming."

Their faces fall in unison and I am reminded, again, that we are not at the same place in our journey.

Having an alcoholic in the family is new to my husband's family. Actually, they've had an alcoholic in the family as long as I have. The difference is that I had a label for my dad 30 years ago, and they are just learning to say Peggy's diagnosis out loud.

In the decade since I joined the family, I've watched their progress. They've danced around Peggy's drinking problem in conversations. When they acknowledged it at all, they would clarify that the problem was only with white wine. They've hosted family gatherings where white wine was conspicuously absent but red wine was plentiful and filled Peggy's glass more than once. They've discounted Peggy's late-night phone calls as quirky and made excuses for her absence.

Now that the truth can no longer be ignored, they have learned to say the words out loud.

Peggy is an alcoholic.

She is an alcoholic on Thanksgiving, and Easter, and Election Day. She is an alcoholic when all is going well and an alcoholic when life is a struggle. Today she is an alcoholic who won't be coming to Christmas dinner because a week ago my mother-in-law dropped her off at a 28-day in-patient treatment program.

"We're not supposed to know," my mother-in-law reminds me.

"But we do," I reply.

"She wants to keep it a secret," my mother-in-law says with an edge of pleading. Peggy wants us to pretend to be surprised when she doesn't show up for dinner. Peggy wants us to pretend to believe her husband when he says she's not feeling well and decided to stay home. And, Peggy's not alone.

Pretending all is well suits my in-laws just fine. It fits their vision of their family. It reflects their wish for what is true. They have circled the wagons, and my insistence on reality is being treated like an angry wolf. They feel threatened. They think I'm being cruel and heartless. They think I don't understand.

But I do.

I lived inside a circle of wagons when I was young. I kept neighbors at a safe distance, told half-truths to clergy and teachers, and made excuses for my absence from daddy/daughter functions.

I spent years pretending not to see the truth. I pretended to believe my father had to cancel our plans because he was working late. I pretended he was just tired. I pretended it was Coke in his cup. I pretended the fabricated versions of events he used to fill in what the blackouts removed were true. I pretended not to fear *that call* when the phone rang late at night.

When I finally got tired of carrying baggage that didn't belong to me, I stopped pretending. It wasn't easy because it meant facing hard truths: My father lied and manipulated. My father cared more about drinking than he did about me. My father was likely to die before I graduated or walked down the aisle or held a baby in my arms. My father was an alcoholic, and I couldn't do anything about it. I didn't cause his addiction, I couldn't control his addiction, and I couldn't cure his addiction.

With time and practice, I learned to step out from behind the circled family wagons. I learned the freedom of refusing to be complicit in the deceit. I learned the peace of not trying to calm the chaos. I learned the joy of flaunting my flaws and imperfections and being loved anyway. I learned to live with messy and uncomfortable truths and I cannot stomach the idea of going back to a life of lies.

So, no. I will not be setting a place for Peggy. I won't pretend I don't see what is right in front of me. I will not be turned into a liar by those who can't acknowledge the truth. I won't contrive calm to compensate for the chaos alcoholism creates.

There is plenty of room in my heart to love Peggy, but there is no room to lie for her.

I will rub eleven china plates with a flour sack towel to remove smudges and place the salad and dinner forks perfectly parallel on each navy napkin. I will welcome our guests with a smile and hug them a little tighter than usual in hopes of easing the pain they are feeling. I will show them to the table where there are just the right number of plates for the guests attending, offer a prayer of thanks for those gathered, and a prayer of healing for those absent.

Then, I will pass the food I've lovingly prepared and hope that next year I will use twelve plates.

Kristina Cerise is a Seattle writer and editor. She grew up in the shadow of her father's alcohol addiction, impacted by his choices far more and far longer than she expected. Kristina is drawn to personal narrative and memoir because there is freedom in telling the whole, messy truth—both to herself and to others. Telling the truth about her damage and desires was what opened the door to the life she's living now: married to the kindest man and raising the greatest kids.

Writing is how Kristina finds meaning in the madness of her past and present. Her writing has appeared in *Working Mother; Creative Nonfiction; Brain, Child;* and most recently in *Motherhood May Cause Drowsiness,* 2nd ed. She blogs about words and what they mean to her at definingmotherhood.wordpress.com and occasionally impersonates a bird @DefineMother.

Get Your Ass to Al-Anon

Chelsea Lai

I booked a redeye flight Vegas-to-Florida because that way, I'd get situated and drift effortlessly into a peaceful slumber for the damn near six-hour flight across the country. Instead I was sardined between two large men, one sawing logs, the other's body mush oozing over and totally invading my personal space. That left me awake, annoyed, and flipping through magazines, trying to chill out. My poor, tiny-pea bladder was like a water balloon primed to burst during the last five hours of the flight since I was trapped in the middle-aged snoozing man sandwich.

On top of the uncomfortable seating situation (compounded with an irrational fear of flying: we're all going to burn!), was the reality felt in the pit of my stomach: I am going to a rehab family weekend. My baby brother is in rehab. I had secretly wished, prayed, hoped, and bargained for him to finally realize he needed help and seek treatment. I was pleased that he had. What I did not sign up for, however, was that I had to partake of this rehab nonsense, even though I was not the one with the issues. Clearly, I was perfect . . . or at least I struggled to be every day of my life so as to not bring about any more stress to my family.

I arrived at Fort Lauderdale at 6 a.m. "This is such a great opportunity, so special to be here," chanted cheerleader Chelsea to crabby pants Chelsea as I bee-lined it to the nearest lavatory, then trudged toward the baggage claim area. Stepping off the escalator, I felt some heart happy sparkles for the first time in about four months. My brother had told me he wouldn't be allowed to come to the airport to pick me up, which pissed me off since I was flying all that way for him. Yet there he was with his big

Tiger Woods–toothed grin, a tan from the Florida sun, and his body in the best shape in years from daily gym visits.

My tears broke out of the floodgate. The last time I had seen him was when he had boarded the plane in Vegas on a (why is it still 100 degrees?) day in September. I truly did not know if I would see him alive again. I had prepared myself for his death many times over; the turmoil and meltdown leading him to rehab had left me broken and uneasy about his future.

"Soooo, how's everything going?" I asked Chad after we smashed my ginormous suitcase into the micro trunk of the rented Chevy Spark and I settled into sardine can #2 of the trip. There was an uncomfortable feeling lingering in the air. A lot had happened since his departure from Vegas three months ago. He had nearly made it through an entire 30-day stint at his inaugural rehab venue—I'm still not sure why he was asked to leave early. Then he had decided to jump ship to Del Ray Beach, where he entered rehab numero dos, found a girl (oh, here we go), and relapsed twice, which leads us to this weekend.

After a pause, Chad said, "Everything is good, sis." It was his always reply, even if things were a total shit storm. But at that point I was merely overjoyed to be driving down the interstate with him. It was the most relaxed I had been in months. I kicked my seat back the whopping two inches allowed in the silver clown car and let myself soak up the new scenery. We rode together toward Del Ray in the glorious sounds of gangster rap.

I had played this family program ordeal out in my imagination for weeks. It would go like this: we'd sit around with other pathetic families obsessing over our out-of-control loved ones. There would be tears, hugging, and worst of all . . . sharing of our feelings. The counselors would hand us tissues along with understanding and sympathetic nods as we embarrassingly told our stories. It was going to be a real disaster.

I already knew I was better than all the people in his rehab group, for sure, probably most of their families as well. I had a college education, a master's degree even. I was an outstanding educator, married to another perfect human. I owned my own home and car, and didn't need to drink or use drugs to have a good time.

"This is really, super nice, your rehab owner doesn't mess around," I joked as I unloaded my belongings in the hotel room.

"Yeah, Dave likes to show the families a nice time when they're here. He thinks it's important since you put up with so much from us."

"You've got that right, this will be weird, but I am really glad to see you at least!"

"Same here. It will be really good, just wait and see. Dave and all the other counselors are pretty amazing. I've learned a lot here. Really good stuff. We better get down to the meeting room, can't be late!"

Poop. Okay. Here we go. We exited the elevator and strolled into the sunlit lobby to meet the rest of the group. I was taken aback by the people I saw. They looked just like my family. Regular, normal, everyday people. Except with an air of anxiety, along with those dark circles under their eyes and chewed cuticles that were all too familiar to me. They were mostly white, middle-aged, and visibly ashamed.

The clients (a nice word for the alcoholic/addicts who were in treatment) were there too, a carefree bunch who were tattooed and pierced, and were smoking, cussing, and drinking Red Bull like it was going to stop production at any moment. Chad and another kid, Matt, were the only clean-cut exceptions. They had bonded over their love of golf and the country club life. Oh, and girls.

"Everyone follow me, please," muttered a bleach-blond young man donning a well-worn Metallica concert tee.

We all glanced at each other with nervous looks as we walked the Green Mile—I mean down the hallway to our assigned conference room. The chairs were set up in a circle. There was an impressive spread of snacks and beverages laid out as well. We filed in, making small talk. Some people grabbed a water or sat right down to check emails on their phones. I meandered over the veggie tray and proceeded to stuff my face with carrot and celery sticks so nobody would try to strike up small talk with me.

Dave (the owner) and the other counselors came glowing into the room. Yes, I said glowing. They were all golden tanned, ultra-white smiled, Tommy Bahama–wearing, freaking happy people.

"Hello! Everyone, please find a seat so we can begin, we have much to cover in these two short days," Dave boomed.

I am pretty sure if he would have said, "Go out the front doors of the hotel, then walk five blocks down the street and straight into the ocean," I would have done as he requested. Dave was tall, dark, and scary, yet I could tell he had kindness in there somewhere as well.

"We are grateful you all traveled to be here for your loved one this weekend. Family support is huge for successful recovery, and without your support it would be much harder. We are going to do a lot of work the next two days, I hope you are prepared to participate just as you expect your loved one to do in group and therapy sessions."

Damn, he was good. Real good. He got me thinking: how could I expect Chad to give it 100 percent day in and day out, if I couldn't do the same? Nothing worse than a hypocrite in my book! I became a tiny bit less skeptical at that point and decided to at least try. I was actually kind of afraid of what Dave would do to me if I didn't act engaged.

We went around and made brief intros. I learned that one mom was extremely distraught over her son's addiction and felt all alone in her suffering; her family and church friends would be appalled if they knew the truth. One father used to drink and smoke weed with his daughter; he didn't realize it was such a problem until she got out of control. Another dad was spiraling deeper into horrible health because he was so worried and stressed about losing his daughter to drugs. Tears would not stop pouring out of the eyes of another mother; she barely got out her name as she was so emotional in the presence of her "baby boy" who grew up to be a drug addict.

These parents had lost jobs, gotten divorced, and were failing to adequately parent their other children because they were entirely fixated on fixing their addict child. I was just a crazy sister who loved her brother and wanted him to clean up his behavior and never drink again. Despite all the varying situations and circumstances, we were all exactly the same. We were utterly obsessed with losing a loved one to dirty, disgusting, life-crushing drugs. Turns out, I realized, the clients were not the only "sick people" in that room.

The initial session involved the family members and the counselors only. The clients were released to go work in their own groups. I was sure the parents were in for an earful about how terribly they had screwed up their children, also that they needed to stop rushing in to the rescue and let their children live independently. I was probably going to be seen as an innocent victim in all of this; the brave sister who held the family together and was losing her soul in the effort.

Instead, we were asked to do some major soul-searching, to find our part in all the chaos, to allow ourselves the dignity of living again. I felt emotionally naked, entirely vulnerable, and utterly terrified. I had spent so many years trying to rescue Chad, I did not even see that I was hurting him more than helping. I had my own truckload of issues, and was completely clueless to them as I sat on my throne and tried to rule Chadsville. I know my mum and stepdad felt the same way. They had flown in from Wyoming for the weekend as well. We hadn't had much time to talk since they arrived, but I could feel the energy emitting from them. We shot knowing looks to the ground as questions posed by the counselors zapped us all right to the core.

Lots of, "How do you feel when ___?" "What do you do when ___?" "What do you think about ___?"

People squirmed in their seats, fidgeted, got up every five minutes for water. We were all clearly in excruciating pain as we talked about our part in everything, our feelings, and our fears. It was terrible. And by terrible I mean enlightening and spiritual in a way I had never experienced. For the first time in my life, I felt connected to other humans on the same level. No judgment, no worry they were going to turn around and laugh at me. Even my parents mentioned they felt oddly united with the other parents, all without saying a word about it. We walked in that morning total, separate strangers, and walked out that afternoon puffy-eyed, emotionally joined friends.

"So, what all did they make you do today?" Chad inquired that evening with a smirk on his face.

"Well, we talked," Mum responded. "Mostly about ourselves. A little bit about you, but mostly ourselves." She seemed too drained to come up with a very detailed answer.

"Yeah, and we even got homework. What the hell!" I chimed in, trying to keep my hard-ass edge.

The homework assignment was fairly simple and upfront. We each had the evening to compose a letter to our loved one. We had to include the following: fears, angers, regrets, hopes, resentments, and happy/sad memories. Doesn't seem so bad, right? Well, here's the kicker: the next day the closing session was going to entail each of us sharing our letters with the entire group. That made me want to throw up on the spot. I have never had a more horrendous case of writer's block than I did that night. Normally, I'd just let it fly. But knowing I had to read this letter to Chad in front of everyone made me hypersensitive and I wanted to crawl into my little Cancerian crab shell. I barely even slept that night, and not because I was afraid Chad was going to steal the Spark keys and make a run for it (totally crossed my mind), rather because I knew what lay ahead. And it was scary. Horrifically scary.

Cut to the next morning at our lovely continental breakfast of Raisin Bran, plain white bagels with plain white cream cheese, and fairly decent coffee (plus a million Red Bulls and cigs for the clients). If physically and spiritually drained had an entry photo in the dictionary of psychology, all of the family members would have made the model cut that day. A sea of crimson, swollen eyes covered up with mascara was accompanied by fresh wrinkles and a few gray hairs I swear were not present the day before. I was exhausted, yet hopeful, kind of hungry, yet not hungry because I felt like I was going have an unfortunate stomach episode in front of everyone.

"Morning. Please, follow me," mumbled our enthusiastic escort from the day prior.

We filed into the conference room of doom and sat right down this time—no time for grazing at the snack table or checking pretend emails. Team Codependent silently reread their letters, some feverishly making last-minute revisions. Nobody appeared cool and confident. It struck me as so comical and ironic that the clients were the only relaxed ones in the room. They joked around and laughed with each other, happy and carefree as pigs in mud.

It had always been like that though: me lying awake at night, heart pumping, waiting for a horrendous-news phone call while Chad ran amuck in the neon lights of Vegas, wasted out of his gourd. Until that moment I hadn't made that realization. I was wasting precious time, stressing myself out, trying to control the uncontrollable. For what? It was getting me nowhere except anxious and leading me to dread the buzz of my phone while living in a future that did not even exist (and probably never would). I wanted to be a happy pig too, dammit.

"Good morning, hope you all slept well!" bellowed Dave. He was already back in action for such an early hour (okay, maybe 9 a.m. isn't that early by most standards).

"Blah, blah, blahhhh, blaaaah, and then we'll share your letters," was all I heard.

The time had come. The scariest, most vulnerable activity of the entire weekend: letter sharing time. The letters were amazingly beautiful, heartfelt, and genuine. Many parents started off recalling the births (or adoptions) of their child (cue waterworks from the first sentences!). They described their precious bundle, their hopes for the future, and continued with stories highlighting the innocence of childhood. They then went into what it felt like to watch that sweet baby self-destruct on a path paved with lying, stealing, and ghastly behavior—all fueled by drugs and alcohol. It was hard for many of them to even speak because the tears were gushing out. I felt like I was watching a Lifetime movie, except a super stellar, non-cheesy one. I was completely shaken down to my core. I knew I would never be able judge a fellow human being again; I did not have that right.

The mom to my right finished her last word and shakily folded up her letter. The spotlight was now burning my flesh. "Chelsea, why don't you go ahead and begin," urged one of the counselors.

Chad and I faced each other and I let it rip.

"I feel like I failed you as a big sister," I read, my voice sounding shrill in my ears. "I wasn't there when I should have been, and maybe things would have been different. I am sorry."

I shared how pissed off I was that he wrecked my cars, stole my money, and manipulated me over and over again. I also told him I was uncommonly proud that he finally was choosing to change his life, and I would support him no matter what.

"I could never give up on my little brother," I vowed. Chad alternated his glances from the floor to my face, but I could tell my words were hitting home with him. Upon my closure, he hugged me, and opened his writing to me. I honestly cannot tell you what he said to me in his letter. I think I was bawling too hard by that point to hear much. I do remember lots of "I am sorry" and "I am trying to change."

My mum and stepdad's letters paralleled the other parents' writings. They also broke my heart just as hard. You could hear the guilt in my mum's voice as she apologized for her and my dad's divorce and for working such long hours during our childhood. The raw anger also was evident as she recalled many nights of worry, stolen money, lies upon lies, and the terrible choices Chad made while he was loaded. One item I vividly remember in my stepdad's letter was when he said he was offended by Chad's language and use of derogatory words. My stepdad is such a kind person who never raises his voice; he definitely got out some pent-up irritations that day. I wanted to clap for him while hanging on the edge of my seat waiting for Chad to flip out. But he didn't. Nobody did. The energy was amazingly calm and positive, even though many people let out their secret feelings that afternoon.

The entire experience of the weekend showed me a different side—that there is far more to addiction than just one individual. We all played a part. I had issues of my own to deal with. The parting gift to all the family members from the counselors was this message: Take care of yourself. We have things under control here. Go home and find an Al-Anon meeting. Find a sponsor. Take care of yourself!

For the first time, the crushing, debilitating reality of addiction and the joyous optimism for recovery became very real to me. I knew I could no longer wake up in the morning and have my first thought be about my brother and his recovery or relapse. Being so anxious and on-edge meant I could barely function. I was a ghost of myself with a fake smile and laugh amidst a head and heart of constant turmoil.

This had to stop, I just wasn't quite sure how. After looking a hot mess, crying alone in the airport, and mulling it over most of the flight home, I decided maybe I could take that advice from the pros. I really did like them, they seemed to know their shit, and at that point I really had nothing to lose besides what little sanity I had left. Back in Fabulous Las Vegas (dripping with sarcasm there), I hopped online to find the Al-Anon meeting schedule for Nevada. I found a meeting at a church close to my house, called Pathways to Recovery. I attended my first meeting that following Wednesday, the 12th of December, 2012.

I remember very clearly walking into the room and wanting to turn and promptly sprint back to the safety of my car. I was by far the youngest one in there, probably by an average of 20 years. My reality: Of course everyone is staring at me, feeling terrible that I married a drunk or had horrid alcoholic parents. Poor, sweet girl! Real reality: Nobody gave a second thought to me being there or judged whatsoever. The meeting started out with the Serenity Prayer. Oh crap. I fell for religious trickery! Then they went onto the steps and traditions. Crap, more G-word! These people were a cult for sure. I had to be on heightened paranoia level so they didn't try to brainwash me!

"Are there any newcomers here this evening for their first, second, or third meeting?" chirped the chipper meeting chair-er woman.

Immediate heat rushed to my cheeks. My head felt as if it would burst into flames. I managed a timid hand raise, and immediately was attacked by an army of smiling faces and kind (but like, real, genuinely kind) eyes staring right at my tomato face.

"Welcome, we'll get you a Newcomer's packet at the conclusion of the meeting," twinkled chair lady with her butter-melting beam.

Next came the sharing of the topic, followed by the members displaying their "experience, strength, and hope." Ew. These people were far too free with their feelings. Yet I was intrigued and felt an undeniable connection to them all, similar to that feeling in Florida. I cannot remember the topic that evening, but what I vividly remember was listening intently to these strong, hard-working, and authentic individuals. Some had grown up in alcoholism, and some married into it and had children involved in the chaos. A few of the members had even lost a loved one to the disease. Yet here they all sat. Still living life, choosing to be happy, not worrying and stressing about uncontrollable things. My stomach began to churn as my turn quickly approached. As a rule, Newcomers aren't expected to share at their first meeting, but I'm an overachiever and needed to impress everyone, so I went for it.

Tears. Welling up like puddles in a rainstorm. Tears. Overflowing down my crimson cheeks. Lots of perspiration as well. Can't leave out that lovely visual.

"I'm Chelsea. I'm here because my brother is in rehab. I don't know what to do anymore, so I'm here. *Pause for some crying* I just want him to be okay."

Those were the hardest few sentences I ever choked out in my life. I was mortified that now the secret was out amongst strangers. The words had left my mouth, never to be stuffed back inside. But surprise: words cannot express the feeling of being in a room where every single person just gets it. No judgment, no criticism, no unheeded advice (which always comes from people who know jack shit about the disease or living with it). We could just *be*, something I had never done in my entire life. I had always been in this sad limbo: sulking in the past and freaking out about the future.

I could not shake that feeling of having utter peace. Nothing could touch me during that hour. I felt exhilarated as I left that evening, even if

I was still a tad bit skeptical with all the God talk. Guess their brainwashing worked because they all told me, "Keep coming back," and I did the very next Wednesday.

I met myriad folks in the program. We were all entirely too similar in our behaviors (controlling, stressing, pushing, stalking, et cetera) and it always made me laugh, while feeling right at home. After a few months, I ventured out to additional meetings. I enjoyed my daily readers very much, and even started some meditation and prayer—to my version of God.

The hardcores were always up my *ah-hem*, saying, "Get a sponsor!"

"Did you get a sponsor yet?!" nosed one hardcore in particular who lived, bled, and died Al-Anon.

"I think you should worry about your own program," I texted in response on one particularly ballsy-feeling evening. Needless to say, I kind of was out of that little group going forward. And I was completely okay with that. My program, my comfort level. I was over trying to impress others and working my buns off to fit in.

I am stubborn, I do things in my own damn time. So, I was pleased with myself for actually attending weekly meetings and reading every day. And I truly was starting to feel much, much better. I also thought it was the bees knees that Chad, my parents, and I could "talk recovery" together. (My parents had also started dabbling in Al-Anon after Florida.) It was a common thread we now shared, rather than Chad going at it solo. After a few months, I started seeing Chad in a new light. I started to leave him alone more, let him take care of his own business. Faith was slowly beginning to creep its way back into my spirit. It was amazingly cool to watch us all start behaving differently, not freaking out as much, controlling anger, not over-dramatizing minute events. We were living healthier, better managed lives.

Roughly six months into my Al-Anon adventure, I had my first true test of recovery. Chad had been sober right around six months and decided it was time to move out of sober living (a place where he lived with other people in recovery) and into his own apartment. He relapsed within a month of being out on his own. Dave and the other counselors had fought tooth and nail to keep Chad in the safety nest of sober living, but Chad used his unparalleled powers of persuasion to get my parents on board with the move. I had seen the writing on the wall, but minded my own business as I was learning to do in Al-Anon.

It was a Sunday afternoon when my phone buzzed and I saw it was my mum calling. My stomach dropped, but I used my tool of gratitude to shout out a quick thanks to my Higher Power that she was alive and healthy enough to make that call to me.

"Well. Your brother has been using for a week or so now. He is a mess. We're not sure what to do, but Dave is going to step in and help."

I could tell she was trying to sound cool and collected. However, the disappointment, fear, and concern were evident in her voice. I felt like I had been sucker-punched by recovery. Wasn't the nightmare all supposed to be over now that we went to programs?! This was total bullshit. All this hard work and for what? For Chad to go out and shoot drugs into his veins (his using had escalated to dilaudid). My heart was crushed into a pulp. The life felt drained out of me, and the remainder of that day and into the evening I lay on the couch by myself, drifting in and out of sleep while Netflix played endless episodes of some outdated sitcom. I fell right back into the attempted control habit of not eating all day and taking on anxiety that was not even from my own turmoil.

I let myself have that one day. After that I knew I had to get back to my practices and keeping myself busy (oh, and eating, too). It was touch and go for the next few weeks. My heart skipped a beat every time the phone rang, and I had a few sleepless nights, but what I noticed was that I no longer let my obsession with him consume my being. I had to credit that to Al-Anon. It kept me hoping, and reassured me that even if something terrible did happen, I would be okay.

It took me about a year of attending meetings, reading, praying, and meditating to prepare myself for taking my recovery to the next step. I felt that I was getting it, but knew I had to give in and get a sponsor for the real magic to happen. There was one lady who had such a soothing voice, and her shares were always what I needed to hear. I walked with her out of a meeting one Sunday afternoon, and almost let her get to her car before I finally gushed, "Do you sponsor? Do you want to sponsor me?" She smiled, replied she had never done it before, but that we could "give it a shot and see what happens." I spent the next year going to her house once a week and working each of the twelve steps in detail. It was all too familiar to family week with my feelings of embarrassment, fear of judgment, and efforts not to get choked up as I shared intimate details of my heart and mind. Each meeting was eye-opening and empowering, and I felt a little stronger with each passing week. My sponsor gave me realistic goals that I could meet. Then, as a team, we walked through the work I had completed. She never nagged me or expected me to dedicate every waking hour to the program. It was the right match and the right time, and our sessions together were greatly valuable.

I would love to say that Chad's recovery has been "perfect" without any bumps in the road. Fortunately that is not how life works (no, fortunately was not a typo). It sounds terrible to be grateful for something as terrible as addiction, but if Chad had never gone into recovery, I never would have either. I would still be an anxious, discontented person wallowing around in a giant pool of my own self-pity. I had a lot of mental garbage that needed taken out to the curb, many behaviors I used as defense mechanisms to keep people from getting too close.

The difference for me now is that if there is a "crisis" I don't freak out and go into panic mode. My brain still tries, believe that, but I am now able to take control of ME and handle my behavior. Without Al-Anon that simply would not be the case. I am becoming a better person in every aspect of my life, leaving Chad alone and giving him the dignity of working on HIS recovery, while being an example of "the change I wish to see in the world." I know, I know, cheese-tastic, but all true! There have been more relapses, lies, and disasters, and always fear lies in wait for a weak moment. Yet I handle each event with more grace than before. I am far from "cured." I still worry and get pangs of random anxiety. The difference is I do not let the feelings come in and take up shop in my brain like I did prior to Al-Anon. I now realize it is fear doing what it does best: attempting to scare the life out of me. I have to practice daily to ensure my faith is grander than my fear. If I slack off, it's unreal how quickly my behavior falls right back into old habits. I also realize no matter how long Chad is sober or if he is not, I will always worry about him somewhere in the back of my heart. He is my little brother, and we are a part of each other whether it's convenient to our sanity or not. We owe it to ourselves to keep up the hard work we've been privileged to experience over the past three years.

Seasoned Al-Anoners suggest trying seven meetings before throwing in the towel, and I am ever so thankful that I took that initial piece of advice. Al-Anon has given me the tools and support I need to keep my hard-earned sane brain, and has taught me that it's all about "progress, not perfection." So if I get nutty, I don't have to beat myself up about it. I know it means I am neglecting some piece of the sanity pie and need to get to work. It only takes a few hours, sometimes days, but I know how to get back to my happy place if I temporarily get lost.

I feel as if I have been given a second chance to not only live a better existence, but also to become a better wife, parent, and friend. I hope I help others along the way by sharing my adventure in Self-Discovery Land (that's a real place, and it's scary, man), especially with those cynical newcomers, who are just like I was, not that long ago. I tease with Chad all the time that we both "drank the Kool-Aid" of Al-Anon and AA, and we liked it, dammit! But all jokes aside, my life has become such a better place to live. I'm certain others around me agree. I think I'll "Keep Coming Back."

Chelsea Lai was born in Casper, Wyoming, and now resides among the glittering lights of Vegas. She has a master's degree in Elementary Education, and has spent the past eight years teaching and inspiring her students to become independent, lifelong learners and lovers of literature. Within the last year, she and her husband, high school sweetheart and fellow Casper native Dan Lai, welcomed their son Andy into the world. With this incredible life change, Chelsea decided to take a step back from teaching in order to put her energy into being with their son, also helping with the recovery movement in her community. She joined a local nonprofit, and is working with a team to bring a sober high school to Las Vegas. During her personal time, she enjoys sharing her own recovery, which parallels that of her younger brother's, on her blog (www.insideacrazybrain.wordpress.com) aiming to educate others about the multiple facets of addiction and the hope of recovery.

Homeland Security

Margaret Smith-Braniff

I had begun to keep my distance
when the bottles began to explode.
I turned to look.
"Get tough," you said.
I'd already begun.

I'd split by the time
the big pieces began to fall.
It was the shards—
microscopic slivers of
sarcasm—that penetrated.

I couldn't move fast enough
I couldn't cover up enough
I couldn't toughen up
enough
to prevent those slices.

You can't touch me
yet.

I have nicks in endless
tiny crevices.

I have shards of the bottle
in places
even I don't expect.

To touch me means:
Go slow.
Find the pieces
wedged and hidden.
Be prepared
to remove them
one by one.

Margaret Smith-Braniff lives a picture-perfect life: a home on the range—on her family's ranch in northern Wyoming. She rises every morning to an amazing view of the Big Horn Mountains, with Crazy Woman Canyon framed by cottonwoods, prairie, and sky. For 25 years, Margaret taught English in the regular classroom but came home to become manager of the family properties, where she began learning grasses, forbs, and weeds instead of teaching essays, stories, and poems. Then she got married. Challenges of love and life exploded—mainly because of alcohol. She still lives what looks like a picture-perfect life with her recovering husband, two dogs, and brazen wildlife, but also with the constant reminders: "One day at a time" and "There truly is a Higher Power."

Family, Interrupted

Patricia McDaniel

Milestones are the markers along life's pathway.

When you are a parent, your child's milestones are the events you eagerly anticipate: the excitement of the first day of kindergarten, watching her make friends and laugh on the playground. Later you look forward to seeing her off on her first date, taking pictures of her in her prom dress, watching her cross the stage at her high school graduation, helping her move into her dorm room at college. These milestones are so important and you cling to them as proof that you have been a "good parent."

I was raised in a home with an alcoholic parent, so I was committed to creating an environment for my children that was devoid of the chaos I had known: my father coming home drunk, surly and irritable, never being able to have friends over because of his unpredictability and fits of verbal rage, keeping an eye out for any indication that he was about to blow. I didn't drink alcohol, didn't smoke, and I tried to be the most engaged and supportive parent I could be. I was present and involved in my children's lives and encouraged them at every turn. I read to them at bedtime. I sent them to wildlife camp, basketball camp, Brownie camp, enrichment excursions, museums, the zoo, the theater, vacation trips. I attended every school concert, every piano recital, every parent-teacher conference, every PTO bazaar and book fair. Maybe I "helicoptered" a bit, but I was determined that my children would never have the scary and insecure childhood I had experienced. Those who do not heed history are bound to repeat it, and I heeded history with a vengeance. I had this—I had it all figured out.

I believed that if I continued to be the best, most loving, most supportive mom I could save my children from the pitfalls of adolescence: drunk driving, teenage pregnancy, unhealthy associations, smoking, drug and alcohol abuse. I was confident that middle-class values would act as a vaccine for my kids, a shot in the arm to prevent social ills from touching them. I didn't expect their lives would be without difficulty—what adolescent's life is?—but I believed they would be the usual, minor adolescent struggles. After all, my husband (their father) and I were professionals, well-educated, successful, respected in our community. We were solid citizens, providing a two-parent home. This was my identity, this was who I was. I had worked hard to earn it and I believed the benefits of my success would surely accrue to my children.

Life was not perfect nor did I expect it to be. I was at times challenged as a parent. It's a well-known fact that children of alcoholic parents tend to be either crisis-oriented as adults, or hyper-responsible with a high need for order and control. I was the latter, and I planned (controlled) my kids' lives, or at least tried to. Nonetheless, my son—a very smart kid—didn't take to school, wouldn't study, and got one of two grades on every paper: either an A or a zero. The A's meant he absorbed the material with very little effort. The zeros meant he just didn't really give a damn. My daughter was socially awkward, alienated, shy, keeping her distance from other children her age. She, too, struggled in school. She had few friends and even those relationships were often strained. She was isolated and preferred to stay home rather than go outside to find someone to play with. I once paid her to go down the street to play with another little girl her age.

My daughter moved into junior high school and kept me up many, many nights worrying, trying to figure out what was wrong with this precious girl that I loved so deeply. Why was everything so hard for her? I did what any responsible parent would do: I found a good counselor to help bring her out of her shell. Sometimes I would go with her, where I learned firsthand how good she was at diverting the counselor from the issue at hand.

When she became a teenager, she was someone I didn't recognize anymore. She was sullen, withdrawn, secretive, then, without warning, enraged and screaming at me, then falling into bouts of extreme sadness.

She would shout expletives at me regardless of where we were or with whom, and come home the next day with flowers, apologizing for being so disrespectful. She stopped washing her hair, she wore baggy shirts to hide her weight loss, her eyes were red, pupils often dilated, and I could hear her rambling around the house at night. She was failing her classes. She threatened to drop out of school. Immediately upon waking every morning, my first thought was what daughter-induced crisis or upheaval I would have to face that day.

Other ominous signs emerged: she was sneaking out, she could not sit in a movie theater for 30 minutes without having to get up and leave for at least 10 minutes, and sometimes she didn't sleep for days. I would see her around town when she was supposed to be at school or at work, often with people I did not know. These people looked older than her and didn't appear to be particularly "prosperous." She continually created crisis in our home and discord with me and with her father. The life I had so carefully constructed was crashing down around my ears.

One spring evening my son came to me with a secret he no longer believed he could—or should—keep. His sister was using meth on a nearly daily basis. She was being supplied with meth by a man in his early 30s at whose home she frequently would hang out. I began to understand that this was behind the violent mood swings, weight loss, lack of sleep, outbursts, and mysterious comings and goings from the house. She had already dropped out of high school and I still hadn't come to grips with the fact that I had been powerless to prevent it. *A high school dropout*: I just couldn't wrap my head around that sad fact. My son finally came forward because her behavior was truly scaring him: she told him she was injecting meth. I heard "inject" and my head was immediately filled with mental pictures of skid row junkies in a dirty back alley in some deteriorating urban neighborhood.

The next three days were . . . hell. Pure and simple. That same night I took her to the emergency room where she recited to the ER doctor her drug history. I was shocked—who *was* this kid, anyway? How could she have lived under my roof and I not know about this? I couldn't help but notice the disapproval bordering on contempt in his voice as he talked with her—directed, I believe, at both of us. She, the delinquent teen, and me, the neglectful, clueless mother. She was then transferred to the Behavioral Health Unit where she was by far the youngest patient and kept in a single room behind the nurses' station to separate her from the rest of the population. She was so young, so small, and so vulnerable. I felt protective of her and also ashamed that as a family we had sunk so low. Clearly it was my fault. I spent nights going over in my head every bad decision, wrong word, inappropriate reaction I had had as a mother that had turned my daughter into a meth addict.

So now what? I had no idea what to do. I knew that my husband's alcoholic mother had received treatment at Harmony in Estes Park, but they wouldn't accept a 15-year-old. Too risky. I was on my own. I found out about Hazelden from a colleague and called them. I'd heard of it only because I'd read that Hazelden was where actresses and rock stars went to get clean. How does one place a child in drug rehab? Do you call and make a reservation? What if they don't take her and I have to bring her home with me? That thought terrified me because I had no idea how to move forward with her knowing what I now knew. I called Hazelden and prayed this would be the miracle to help my child. I was so desperate I didn't even think to ask about the cost, which by the way turned out to be A LOT. Within 48 hours she was on a plane to Minneapolis, Minnesota, where she would be met by a member of the Hazelden staff at the door of the plane and transported to the facility. The flight had to be nonstop and her father had to watch her *get on the plane* so she couldn't run. By now, she was out of her drug-induced high and pissed off. She had no interest whatsoever in going to treatment. As luck would have it, this was long before 9/11 and you could accompany your loved one all the way to the gate. She was furious with me and at being forced to go into treatment. My only leverage—my ONLY leverage—was that she was a minor.

My daughter was just three months shy of her 16th birthday. It would be three long years before she returned home. It was good thing I didn't know this at the time, or I would never have let her go.

I was overwhelmed by every kind of emotion: fear, grief, disappointment, confusion, but mostly anger. Her father and I were both angry and outraged. Angry, and really truly pissed off at our daughter. I gave her everything. I provided stability, consistency, a comfortable life, love, support, attention, and yet she betrayed me by becoming a drug addict? She completely disrupted my comfortably constructed life. Don't drug addicts come from poor homes with unstable, broken families?

How dare she do such a thing to me?

I was still angry when my husband and I boarded the plane to Minnesota three weeks later to participate in Hazelden's family program. Angry, embarrassed, and fearful that our friends and associates would find out what was going on in our family. It has to be the parents' fault, right? I had to have done something terribly wrong for this to have happened. When we arrived, she didn't greet us so much as sneer at us with contempt. It was not the reunion *or the apology* I certainly felt I was due. But something unexpected happened to me (and her father) in Minneapolis, at Hazelden. Something truly remarkable. Something that helped me to rid myself of the anger and start the journey toward understanding and empathy. This didn't happen in the span of a day or a week, but it happened slowly, over time. I won't say I came home from Minnesota no longer angry and no longer embarrassed. But I was beginning to see the situation differently. I learned about the disease of addiction. I learned that anger was the least helpful response to what was happening to my child. Most importantly, I was seeing that there were many families affected as ours was and the suffering out there is immense.

For the first time, I met families who were going through what I was going through. The stories were so similar, they were mirror images of my experiences. Before this I was in a private anguish, making excuses in order to keep our shameful secret from our friends and community. Ironically, they were the same secrets my mother, sister, and I worked hard to keep about our father's alcoholism. For the first time I actually laughed out loud as I shared with other parents the absurd and ridiculous situations my daughter had put me in. How could I have been so blind, so dumb, so unaware?

I began to understand that the disease of addiction caused the behaviors and that the disease was chronic, insidious, crafty, ever-present, and *treatable*. As my husband and I shared our pain with each other and the group facilitator, I tearfully talked about all the milestones I would never see accomplished: no prom, no graduation, no graceful transition from high school to college, no celebrations of successes. Okay, so maybe that was shallow, but what parent doesn't have these dreams and plans for their child? They are very hard to let go of. But this was not about *me*. My daughter was alive and in a place of hope, and that was a gift. Perhaps she had a future after all.

The road ahead was not an easy one, nor was it cheap: she would spend 30 days at Hazelden, then another six months in a long-term facility in Rochester, Minnesota. She would then remain in the community of Rochester for another year of aftercare including participation in a twelve-step program. The tab for treatment alone was in excess of $70,000, which we paid out of pocket because the insurance company refused to cover it. She made some missteps—none fatal—although for some of the women she had come to know from treatment, death *was* the inevitable outcome. She began to understand that, yes, this disease will kill you if you don't pay attention. She resisted treatment for several months, and there were times I was really, really scared she wouldn't make it. I threatened dire consequences if she did not stay in treatment and address her disease, all the while knowing that ultimately it would be up to her. There are things you cannot make your children do: you can't make them go to sleep, you can't make them eat, and you cannot make them do their homework—or actively participate in drug treatment.

My daughter was blessed with an outstanding counselor, Sandy, who kept her on target, gave her no slack, and didn't cut me any, either. Sandy permitted no excuses, no casting of blame, no enabling. In her newly found sobriety, my daughter didn't always make the best decisions. But she prevailed. She made it. While I give much credit to Hazelden, The Gables, and to Sandy, I have to give full credit to my girl: treatment is hard, lonely, and it can be brutal and self-affronting, but her 16-year-old self did it. I have often wondered if I could have done it, had the situation been reversed.

At 18 she returned home to Wyoming and to her family. Even though I had visited her many times in those three years, it pained me that we had been separated for so long. The daughter I knew, when not under the influence of drugs, could be funny, insightful, joyful, and full of laughter. I had greatly missed that. I had not been able to watch her daily as she grew, and yet, the young woman who returned to me was truly remarkable. I could not believe the depth of her courage. I could not believe her strength and determination. I was in awe.

How was I changed? How were my husband and I changed as a married couple? We decided to open up about our family's situation and quickly learned that in so doing other families were encouraged to open up as well. We were not ashamed of our daughter and her circumstance was no longer a secret. And while we didn't broadcast her situation gratuitously to the world—that would have been disrespectful to her and unfair—we also didn't shrink from talking opening about it with other struggling families. We were surprised to learn the sheer number of families who were impacted by the addictions of a close family member.

We decided to learn all we could about addiction and the current science, research, and promising treatment modalities. We learned that a 30-day program is only a detoxification, that most addicts require at least six months of intensive in-patient treatment to begin to get a handle on their disease, and that aftercare and peer support are absolutely critical to staying in recovery. One stint in treatment is often not enough. We learned that the disease of addiction is no different than the disease of diabetes in that it is a chronic condition that requires daily monitoring and support.

We became convinced that it was critically important to take this message to the wider community. My husband shifted his professional focus to the treatment and de-stigmatization of addiction and prevailed upon our governor to allow him to collaborate with the best experts in addiction research to write the blueprint for the State of Wyoming, one that would guide all state-funded substance abuse programs going forward. A social worker by profession, I began to volunteer in the county jail and established a support group for female inmates, the majority of whom were incarcerated for drug- or alcohol-related offenses. I saw in their faces the face of my daughter, and understood how fortunate we as her parents had been to be able to intervene during her teen years. Unlike many families, we had also been blessed with the ability to meet the expenses of her treatment. It could all have so easily gone the other way.

Milestones are the markers along life's pathway.

My daughter will be 35 years old next month. Twenty years have passed since she entered treatment. There have been so many milestones since then: marriage, children, a solid career, friendships, higher education. Like all of us, her life has its ups and downs, but it is a good life filled with purpose and joy. Most of her friends today don't know about her experience because they met her long after that time in her life, but she won't shy away from talking about it if asked. She is a strong woman who applies the lessons she learned in treatment to every aspect of her life today.

Before all this happened, I had a tendency to be judgmental. At one time I thought that if a kid was a mess, it must be because the parents are a mess, or someone dropped the ball somewhere. A very wise older woman once told me, "If you have kids, anything can happen. Anything. So you better be prepared. And you better not judge."

Now, I never judge.

Patricia McDaniel is a social worker by profession and a committed community advocate. She has worked in public and private child welfare agencies with children in foster care and with foster and adoptive families. Patricia and her husband established the first Habitat for Humanity affiliate in Wyoming and served as National Administrators for Habitat for Humanity in Nicaragua. Patricia is a former member of the Board of Directors of Wyoming's only Recovery Community Organization, Recover Wyoming. The mother of two grown children and grandmother of five, Patricia lives in Laramie, where she continues to be an advocate for at-risk youth and individuals in recovery.

With All Due Respect

Lynn G. Carlson

Normally, I love the drive from Laramie, Wyoming, to Sheridan: the winding turns of Sybille Canyon, and later, the Big Horn Mountains, deep gray and lavender with chocks of white. But not today.

Just this morning I was curling my hair and thinking how peaceful it is when my sister Laura, two years older than me, is tucked away in a substance abuse treatment center. Then I shook a finger at myself in the mirror. *Shame on you, Lynn.*

Later on, the phone rang. A counselor from the center, introducing herself as Judy, said, "Your sister has chosen to leave treatment." Blunt and to the point she was—a result of much practice at these kinds of phone calls, I suppose.

"Where is she?" I asked.

"Apparently she went to the bar after she left yesterday," Judy said. "One of the counselors went to check on her. She's got a room at the Best Value Motel." When I said nothing, she went on. "Laura listed you as her contact person. She's in room one-oh-four."

I scribbled it down. "So . . . you're done with her then?" I asked, not in a sarcastic tone, simply wanting to verify the baton was being passed to me in this relay race that is my sister's alcoholism.

"Well, once she chooses to leave and drink, we can't have her back in the program." Judy's voice faltered a little. "It's—not fair to the others, you know."

"Of course, I know about that. About the rules and all." And I do know about the rules. This isn't Laura's first rodeo. In the seven years since she started drinking heavily at age 30, Laura has been to treatment four times. But she never left early before. She'd always been the model client, participating enthusiastically, graduating, then attending the requisite 90 AA meetings in 90 days, sometimes even though she'd already started drinking again. We're nothing in my family if not good, obedient students.

"I'll come and get her," I said. "I appreciate all you've done to try and help her." My voice held tears and panic, and I'm sure Judy heard it all. Like she's heard it all before.

"Good luck," she said, with no trace of sarcasm in her voice either.

I was on the road within an hour. I'm very practiced at turning on a dime for rescue situations involving my sister. First I called Mike, my husband of six months, to fill him in. "Watch the weather," he said. "The wind's supposed to kick up, so the roads could get a little dicey." I gave him a mental hug to thank him for his patience. This tall, gentle man had no clue what chaos he was in for when he married me.

As I zip through the curves of Sybille Canyon I wonder what Laura will do next. She keeps getting jobs, then losing them. She's spent most of her retirement funds. Is there even any illusion that she'll stay sober this time?

The other times Laura went through treatment were followed by a honeymoon period where we the family (me, Mom, our oldest sister Sally, and Dad) expressed our faith in her ability to stay sober. Laura basked in that. The honeymoon even lasted a whole 18 months one time and I thought the insanity was over. Until it wasn't.

North of Casper the roads are streaked with black ice. I think of Laura and shake my head. Of the two of us, she's the brighter light, the extrovert, the funny one. She inherited our father's political charisma and love of being front and center. After she left her confining marriage and went back to the University of Wyoming, two kids in tow, she found her calling in a part-time job at the Adult Student Center. She loved helping older students succeed on campus. After graduation she became the director, and the center blazed with activity. It all seemed so natural for Laura, which made the growing attraction to alcohol even more bizarre — it only dims the light and what good is that?

Past Buffalo, the wind grabs my car and jerks it onto the rumble strips. I hate that sound, but it forces me to focus — a good thing because a ground blizzard is starting up. Bands of gauzelike snow shiver over the road and I keep checking the reflector poles to stay in my lane.

Finally I see the exit for Sheridan and pull onto Fifth Street. I spot the Best Value Motel and as I slow down for the left-hand turn, I notice the Jule's Bar and Liquor sign off to the left of the motel parking lot. Should have known Laura'd bunk close to the well, the source of her oblivion. I pull into a parking space in the crook of the L-shaped motel, in front of room 104.

I get out, stretch my cramped legs, and check the window for signs of occupation. The curtains are closed. I knock, hoping that Counselor Judy has the number right. No answer. I knock louder. Nothing. She could be passed out in there. Or, she could be over at Jule's place.

I cross the parking lot, stepping around puddles. The February sun has dropped behind the two-story balconied section of the motel and the puddles are starting to ice over. Soon this stretch of cement will be a skating rink.

Outside the bar, the odor of diesel emanates from mud-splattered trucks. A Coors sign blinks in the window. The place is surprisingly busy for a Tuesday afternoon, probably people in from the oil and gas fields. Inside, some men at the bar turn to see who's coming through the door. I scan the room and know instantly that Laura is not here—nothing but a bunch of Carhartts and brown Budweiser bottles. Hell, what was I thinking? Laura hasn't hung out in bars for years. It's too risky when you're trying to present to the world the face of a recovering alcoholic. No, she drinks at home, alone.

She could be stocking up in the packaged liquor section though, so I head for the door that connects the bar with the liquor store. "Leaving so soon?" says a bearded man at the bar, tipping back his cap with the Mountain Hotshot logo. "You oughtta stay and have a drink with us." He pats the bar stool next to him. I give him a weak smile and peek into the liquor store. No Laura. I head out the way I came in, cross the ever-more-frozen parking lot, and pound on room 104. Nothing.

The bell dings as I push open the door to the motel office. A woman wearing an apron over a UW Cowboys sweatshirt comes in from the living quarters at the back. "Need a room?" she asks.

"Well, no. I've got one." I try to sound confident. "My sister got us a room yesterday. Room 104. But she must be out. She's not answering the door. I just drove in from Laramie, and the roads are getting *really* bad. Ground blizzard. Visibility's terrible. I bet they close the interstate tonight." Ugh. Stop babbling—cut to the chase. "So . . . I need a key to room one-oh-four, please."

The woman sets her lips in a firm line. "We're really not supposed to hand out keys to rooms like that. Unless the person who checks in leaves a name." She riffles through some papers on the counter. "Person in room one-oh-four didn't leave a name." We stare at each other for a moment. "If you want, I can call the room?" The woman dials and holds the receiver to her ear as she smooths her apron. After many rings, she sets the receiver down. "Nobody home, I guess."

I close my eyes. I'm tired from the drive. I'm tired of always dealing with Laura. Sucking in a fragmented breath, I open my eyes. The woman is looking at me, her head tilted slightly. I get hope from the way her lips are not so set anymore and rally to the cause.

"Listen, ma'am. I'm not trying to make trouble, really. Just tell me, the woman in that room, what kind of shape was she in when she arrived? I mean, I'm thinking she was probably pretty drunk?"

The woman hesitates, then nods.

"Well, I'm her sister and I've come to collect her. She left the treatment center up on Third Street. I need to get her back to Laramie. Not tonight. Tomorrow. But I can't do that if I can't get in her room. She's probably passed out in there."

The woman looks away, nods again, then reaches under the counter and extracts a key. She holds it out and says, "She paid for two nights. Check out time's eleven o'clock."

Room 104 is dark. I flip the light switch. Laura is curled up on the couch, her back to the room, shoes on her feet. She's wearing her coat although the room is stuffy-hot. I stand completely still, as I have so many times, and listen. Listen for the sound of her breath. I don't even want to see her face or touch her, until I hear that sound.

Yes, it's there, barely audible over the hum and rumble of the wall heater. I take off my coat, cross the room, and kneel down next to Laura. Immediately I smell vodka-infused sweat. I give her shoulder a light shake. "Laura?" Nothing. I shake harder. "Laura . . . wake up."

"Whaaa . . . what?" She turns her head and looks at the ceiling. Her eyes roam in search of a focus. Slowly she sits up and her eyes finally connect with my face. "Heeey . . . hi." She wipes away some spit that has congealed at the corner of her mouth and scans the room. I can tell she doesn't know where she is.

"You're in Sheridan, Laura. At a motel. You left the treatment center. Do you remember?"

Laura peels off her coat. "Yeah. I remember."

"Well, do you remember *why*?" I'm getting pissed off, now that I see she's all right.

"Why what?"

"Why you left treatment early. I mean, why would you *do* that?"

Laura lists forward. I look around the room. On the bed are three plastic sacks, stuffed with clothes. There's an empty fifth of vodka on the nightstand. I march over, grab it, and shake it at my sister. "So you could have this?" Laura closes her eyes to shut me out. But I'm riled up. I break the cardinal rule (one it took me a long time to get) that you don't lecture, bargain with, or otherwise converse with somebody who's drunk. Big waste of time and breath. I wave the bottle some more. "Dammit, Laura!"

She struggles to her feet. Her jeans are torn at the knee and I know that she has taken a header somewhere. I'm filled with the impulse to get a washcloth and clean up what will be some nasty scrapes on her knees. Laura's face is flushed and distorted. She sways, arms held out in front of her body as if to touch an invisible wall.

"Oh, Jeesus, why don't you lay down before you fall down." I'm done with the anger.

In the bathroom, I toss the bottle in the trash and hold a washcloth under the faucet. After waiting what seems like forever for the water to get hot, I wring out the cloth and carry it to Laura. Who is no longer there.

Cold air pours in through the open door. I drop the washcloth and run outside. It's dark now, but I make out Laura's form in the parking lot, still with her arms held out in front—a short, pear-shaped Frankenstein. She is walk-sliding across the icy asphalt, toward the bar.

"Laura!" I yell. "Come on. Get back in here." I head toward her, adopting the same walk-sliding routine, and try to estimate how far until I intercept her. When she starts to fall, I am helpless to stop her— completely inadequate to the task. Her legs go up in the air, and she lands on her back, arms still out in front.

When I reach her, she is starting to get her breath back. "Are you okay?" I ask. She smiles. Maybe it's the cold air, maybe it's the impact of the fall, but I know suddenly that she is back. My sister has cleared the vodka-fog and is now grinning up at me. She lowers her arms and lies spread-eagled on the ice.

"Hey there, little sister," she says. "I think I fell down."

"Yeah, you did. You okay? Can you get up?"

"Oh, yeah." She rolls over to her side, then onto all fours. She shakes her head when I try to put my hand under her armpit. Laura likes to get up on her own. She pulls her right leg under her and sets the foot on the ground. Pushing with her arms, she rises up enough to get her left leg under her, and pauses to steady herself in this four-point stance. Then she heaves up into a standing position, and tests her balance by moving from foot to foot. "It's cold out here," she says.

"Yeah, *freezing*. Let's get inside." We hook arms and start on the slippery path back to room 104. The streetlight creates a two-headed-monster shadow on the ice that shuffles along in front of us.

"Woo-hoo!" Voices come from above. "Hey there, ladies!" Laura and I stop and look up. Four guys hang over the edge of the motel balcony. "You wanna party?"

"No thanks," I yell. Laura waves at them. I pull on her arm and we continue on our icy trek back to the room.

"But we got beer!" the guy yells.

"Lots of beer!" says another.

Laura and I start to giggle. By the time we make it to the room (the door still open, thank God) we are full-blown howling. I jerk the door shut behind us and we collapse on the bed.

After we catch our breath, Laura curls up on her side, watching me. She strokes the floral bedspread with her fingers. "Are you mad?" she asks. Her beautiful green-brown eyes beg.

"I could kill you," I say, triggering more giggles. Laughter has been our sister bond for as long as I can remember. It was the glue that held us together after Mom left, and then when Dad moved us to a new town and all we had was each other. If we can laugh, we can survive anything.

"I want to see my boy," Laura says as soon as she can talk again. "I *need* to see him, to get my hands on him. Can you take me to Evanston?"

Laura's son has lived with his father in Evanston for almost a year now. He made the decision himself to leave Laramie, to quit living in his mother's house of confusion. He told her, "I deserve to have some happy memories of my high school years."

"We'll see," I say, and I think of Mike and our two dogs back in Laramie and our little house with its warm kitchen. Laura holds her hands out in front of her. They shake. "You need food," I say firmly. "I'll go to Arby's." Laura looks at me, then at the door. No way I should leave her alone, she'll get another bottle. "We'll both go," I say.

She nods. "First I need a shower."

"We need to clean up your bloody knees," I say.

Later, after we finish our sandwiches and potato cakes back in the room, and after I call Mike, Laura holds out her hands again. They're still shaking, but not as bad. "Can you take me to a meeting?" she asks.

"What time does it start?"

"There's one at eight o'clock. What time is it now?"

I check the clock by the bed. "Almost seven-thirty. We can make it."

"A meeting would be good," Laura says.

And it was good. There was comfort there for my sister, in the familiar clank of metal chairs being set out in a circle, in the murmur of "Hi, Laura." She tells the group of her terror at getting sucked back down by the beast and receives simple words of encouragement to fight back, again.

When Laura wakes up in the morning I say what I've been rehearsing in my mind for over an hour. "We can't go to Evanston, Laura. We need to get back to Laramie. I need to go home."

"Oh," Laura says. "Okay." I feel her disappointment. There was a time when I would have driven her all the way across the state, just because she asked me to, and because I'd do anything to distract her from her cravings. So, why *don't* I take her to Evanston?

Because. Because I deserve a life that doesn't involve all the intense watching (Is she drunk? Is she going to try to drive the car?) and the post-binge trips to the grocery store to buy Pedialyte to combat Laura's dehydration. Because I have a new marriage to tend to. Because after trying so many, many times, I finally understand: there isn't a damned thing I can do—any action I can take—that will keep Laura sober.

We gas up the car and get on the interstate. The ground blizzard left behind patches of ice so I focus on the feel of the steering wheel in my hands and think about what Mike told me about how to steer out of a slide, instead of hitting the brakes.

Laura's quite chatty. She talks about the treatment center, the counselors, and other clients. "Meth is a *huge* problem in Wyoming. You should see some of these women—their teeth are falling out and they have horrible marks on their faces. I'm just so grateful I never got hooked on meth."

I want to laugh. I want to slap her. What I do is grip the wheel, sit up straight, and say, "With all due respect, Laura, alcohol isn't doing you any favors."

"Mmm," Laura says. She turns and looks out the window at the Big Horn Mountains. She slumps in her seat, shrinking away from me. I ache for her, but for once I don't make nice and I don't take it back.

"With All Due Respect" first appeared in Northern Colorado Writer's Pooled Ink.

Lynn G. Carlson is the editor of *Watch My Rising: A Recovery Anthology.* She is also a writer and blogger (www.writingwyoming.com) who lives on the prairie outside of Cheyenne, Wyoming, with a retired firefighter, a span-triever, and plenty of gophers. She has published fiction and nonfiction in various literary magazines and online, including a blog post titled "The Top 5 Ways to Sabotage Your Loved One's Recovery" on the Faces and Voices of Recovery blog.

Lynn volunteers with Recover Wyoming as a Recovery Coach, where she provides a listening ear and empathetic heart to family members of people seeking long-term recovery. In 2015, Lynn received a Starfish Award from the Recover Wyoming board of directors in recognition of her work with that organization. One of Lynn's greatest blessings in life is seeing her sister, Laura Griffith, Executive Director of Recover Wyoming, more than 13 years sober and happy as she helps others exit from the chaos of addiction and enter a new life in recovery.

Chile Roasting Season

A. Z. Roa

1. New York, the Mid-Atlantic

When we leave Brooklyn I open the cargo door, and Ray crawls head first into the back of the Jeep. My Jamaican neighbors on Church Avenue look and mutter, then chuckle as they walk past. I leave the Wrangler's soft top on, the plastic windows all zipped and closed shut.

"Failure to plan, plan to fail," he says in a sing-song voice. "The change in environment will do me good," he assures me.

My memory of the roadtrip starts with an image: Brixton, my border collie, sits in the front passenger seat, his white left paw resting on top of my hand. We look like we're going to shift into third gear and accelerate. We are on the Brooklyn-Queens border, heading west and out of New York. Days from now, my husband, two dogs, and I will be on a long stretch of Highway 40, purple skies in Sandoval County, New Mexico.

I text a quick note—"the Dog is my co-pilot"—on my phone and upload our picture onto my dog's Instagram page. My husband, Ray, took that shot of our silhouettes while he was propped up and leaning his back against the cargo door. I've cropped the silhouette so you can see the horizon, not the crooked line that Ray shot. It's not intentionally distorted, but when he drinks, he holds my iPhone upside down, and makes the simplest of point-and-shoot tasks complicated. There are no even horizon lines in his photos of late, only wrecked ones.

Ray is tagging along on this trip because he's afraid to be home all by his lonesome for a month. He is a quiet person, a loner, but I didn't see this aspect of his personality until well after we were living together in that dust-filled, dark railroad apartment in Flatbush. Dust all over the wood furniture he built in his shop. Ray is an artist, but by day he has a stable job as a welder with the Housing Authority, one of the biggest New York City bureaucracies. He snagged the job right after dropping out of art school, so ten years later and with his seniority he takes weeks off work at a time. I write when I'm not working as a rental agent, finding apartments for trust fund babies in newly gentrified places like Prospect Heights, and selling them on the fact that everyone wants to move to Brooklyn nowadays.

Every year Ray and I share the same sad realization that other creative urbanites have here: that most of our savings goes out every month just surviving in New York City. I know that is part of the reason why he drinks. His NYC reality is overwhelming.

I won't let that epiphany bother me now, though, because I am two commission checks richer and with the bills out of the way, I'm roadtripping it and due to arrive in New Mexico with Buddy, a six-year-old pit bull/mastiff. He's from the Brooklyn Animal Coalition Shelter, where I volunteer. He is gentle, has the face of a sad dog who's seen his share of some really horrible basements, I imagine. He had the bad misfortune of getting lumped together with unadoptable fighting dogs, and he would've been euthanized to make room for smaller dogs. Fortunately his waiting owners are my former neighbors, Michelle and Lou, new retirees who moved in the spring to Albuquerque from our Crown Heights neighborhood. They adopted him right before they left, but didn't have room in the car to take him along. I decide to make a long trip out of Buddy's transport, since I haven't done a cross-country trip in a few years. I tell Ray he could come along but he'd have to share the back of the car with the friendly 90-pound dog. Brixton will sit in front. Ray said sitting in front for long periods of time makes his legs go to sleep anyway, so he agreed, and gave me the thumbs up.

The weather is mild and sunny when we get to the outskirts of New Jersey and enter Pennsylvania late in the afternoon. A sign off the road advertises a clean and family-oriented campground, right off Old 22 East in Swatara Township. A toothless woman identifies herself as the caretaker and comes to greet us, takes our $40, and grabs a map from her office. She's escorting us to our site, and because Ray is in a chatty mood, they walk over to the spot a few hundred feet away while I follow in the Wrangler, off to a quiet corner of the campground. When we get to the corner site I see that we are edged between endless rows of withering cornfield on one side, and RVs parked on the other. They're all hitched to electric and water supply posts. One camper has a small three- by five-foot tomato patch, the climbing vines reaching, curling over makeshift wire cages. A woman in a faded cotton housecoat comes out of her trailer with a plastic bucket, begins to water her plants as she watches us drive in. Before she returns to her office Toothless Lady introduces us to our neighbor, a smiling, axe-wielding, plaid-shirted man named Harry. He also has a toothless grin. His blue eyes gleam.

"Nice to meetcha!" he says, extending his hand to my husband. Ray tells him he last pitched a tent in the army and Harry offers to help.

"There's been great ahhd-vahnces in tentistry, no worries," I tell him, as I pull apart semi-attached posts. Harry politely leaves us to settle in. I secure elastic ties into poles, forming the tent frame in five minutes flat. Ray pushes the stakes into the ground and grabs a rock, pounding the metal into the ground so we have secure shelter for the night. I tell him that I hope we're back on the road before sunrise, and to not worry about stabilizing the two-man tent. I just want to crash and don't feel like getting to know these permanent renters.

In the evening he unzips the tent screen and crawls out. I hear Ray moving about in the back of the Jeep. He is making a call, and he roars with anger, followed by crying spells that make it difficult for him to finish sentences without bursting into tears. I believe he's called his therapist, a woman whose services are barely covered by our insurance. It's 10:30 p.m. though, so I know he is having a conversation with her answering machine. Brixton guards the zipper opening of my tent, and watches me for a command.

Later that night as I'm dozing off to sleep, I hear the rumble of motorcycles in the distance. There is evening chatter by the fire, more circling and revving of engines. Through the tent I can make out kerosene lamps floating in the darkness. Whatever is left of my husband's skills as an artist are rarely in evidence these days. He just goes off on a whim, many times inspired by random thoughts. Ray, hearing the laughter in the distance, heads toward the noise and Brixton whines. He can see my husband wandering off from our campsite, but I don't bother calling after him, because intoxicated he only hears voices unfamiliar to me. I get up, out of the tent, to the back of my car. Pointing a flashlight to the trunk I lift up the hidden cargo compartment, and there's an open container of the cheapest, rot-gutting vodka. Fuck.

I step over my dog at the entrance of our tent and crawl back inside. It doesn't take me long to go to sleep. I've discovered the futility of chasing down Ray all the time when he's like this. I'm confident that someone on the grounds will eventually lead Ray back to our site. He's friendly to total strangers when he drinks, and the last thing he wants me to do is to stop him from making friends.

2. The Midwest

I tell Ray to take as many photos as he wants to distract him. He wants to drive, says he's done it many times driving buzzed down Atlantic Avenue back home.

"Two shots," he says. "I've driven home like this, for two years, and you didn't even know. Never stopped by a cop. Not once." I ignore his demands and tell him I can handle the drive.

In a short while though, he begins to feel sick. I look in my rearview mirror and he is pale gray. He says, "We have to find a spot. I thought I could be okay without but I can't."

"Could you at least wait until we get to a city—St. Louis, maybe? The map on my phone says we're in Monroe, Ohio."

"Hell fucking no!" he shouts. Then he whimpers and cries. There's expletives, incessant babbling about Ray Sr., his estranged, deceased father, who's a Latino version of an aging John Wayne. I've heard this story many times before. He escapes from his nursing home, starts drinking heavily again and in less than a month they find his body by a dumpster in Queens. Ray doesn't attend his funeral. No one in his fractured family does, because he had no ID on him, and no criminal record for cops to trace. To Ray, he was just a garden variety drunk, fallen on very hard times. We think he's buried in a remote pauper's grave on the outskirts of the city.

I get off Hwy 40 and now I'm on I-470 heading west along another endless cornfield. We shout at each other, and he begins to dry heave as I turn off the road. Stopping at a tiny market with one working gas pump, he runs inside as if looking for a place to vomit. I'm ambivalent, but I follow him, and inside the Pakistani store clerk gives me the directions I need: keep following the road, past the train tracks and the Walmart. A liquor store will be on my left. She looks at both of us, then rolls her eyes at me. I catch her shaking her head as she turns toward the restroom to anticipate the mess Ray left. It's 11:00 a.m., and although I am a stranger to her, I imagine she knows my shame: that I am about to help my husband get his fix. I brush past Ray who's looking paler than ever, and with my cheeks aflame I open the cargo door and he crawls back inside.

Almost ten miles into the drive I pull in front of Sam's Liquor Stop. I let Ray out the back and an empty plastic bottle rolls out onto the ground. He skips over it, and runs inside the store. Within minutes he returns, and inside the car he pours the vodka down his throat. Ray closes his eyes and then is calm. I'm so mad I still consider leashing him. Maybe I could tether him by a bungee cord to a hook or something that will anchor him. The trembling ceases for now.

"You know," he says, "we have money. We don't have to camp. I just wanted you to be able to say that we did." He starts singing along to The Police. That's all he will listen to, the Da Do Do Da song, for miles and miles, and now I can forget about entertaining the thought of listening to an audio book.

Ray takes shots of the famous Gateway Arch as I zip through St. Louis. It's the end of summer, still hot and muggy, and the shots he takes in our moving car are filled with clouds. At a random gas stop I post the picture of that Arch online. Beads of water begin to distort the side view mirror. The dogs are bored and sleepy.

3. Oklahoma, the Southwest
Raindrops fall as we make a stop for fast food. I know I am heading west when I see a Jack in the Box restaurant every fifth highway food stop. I remind Ray this is what I grew up eating in Los Angeles. My comfort food. I order a Bacon Ultimate Cheeseburger with seven jalapeño poppers. I tell him, "Remember that photo you took of me in San Diego the winter after we met? The overexposed black and white, underneath the sign as I clutched a supersized drink with my fries? My nails were manicured back then, the deepest, darkest claret."

He has no recollection of such events, and instead he closes his eyes and sleeps.

My thoughts drift to an ex-boyfriend, who was originally from Oklahoma. He was a personal trainer, hustling for work in Los Angeles, but eventually ran out of money and went back home to his family's dirt farm in Norman. I heard he lives in Oklahoma City now, born again, and I could easily look him up. I stop at a Petco for some rawhide, and it is not long before I ache to leave this nondescript part of Oklahoma City with its sprawling shopping malls. Back on the highway I am nearly driven off an exit by an aggressive driver in a Land Rover. I decide to keep going until we are well outside the city limits, until the roads morph from asphalt off-ramps, into the red clay dirt of the Cherokee Nation.

4. Sedona, Arizona

There is no magic. The New Age psychics in the tacky, overpriced gem and mineral shops would have you believe otherwise, but instead, there is beauty. Natural beauty in the red sandstone formations, giant red rocks jutting out toward the bluest of blue skies. The Hohokam peoples once called the canyon boulders "sleeping monsters" that guard this small valley nestled in the Coconino Forest.

Instead of magic, there is a man, walking in the middle of town as the sun is setting. He is lost, looking at the tourists who are window shopping before him with great suspicion. He crosses the main drag, Highway 89, and heads down a hill toward more gem shops and hotels.

I catch a glimpse of him from my passenger side window. He doesn't notice the gray Jeep, or the two dogs that whiz by, passing him by ten, maybe fifteen feet. He's stumbling forward, and if you didn't know my husband, you'd think him mad, or at the very least, one of those sleeping giants the ancients speak of. Irritated by the deep, choppy rumblings of a passing motorcycle's exhaust, Ray flinches and covers his ears. He is looking for our hotel, the El Portal, after deciding to play hide and seek in a parking garage in town. He runs into another liquor store, babbling, and I lose sight of him as I turn around a bend.

It was almost an hour ago, and I was in the middle of the busiest part of the shopping strip in Sedona, when I pulled into a parking garage hoping to find a quick bite to eat. Opening the back door, Ray jumped out with his duffle bag, and ran across the parking garage, screaming something about the need to get away from this place. He disappeared around a corner. I decided not to chase after him. I waited. I sat in the car, in the crowded garage for twenty minutes.

I am startled when a woman in a Benz honks at me, and politely asks if I am leaving. I start the engine and wished there were mystical healing powers that were present here. I wished that the so-called energy vortex of the Bell Rock boulders could convince my husband to come back to his family. Instead, the power of Georgi vodka took hold. Ray no longer self-medicates to keep "voices and anxieties" at bay. According to Ray I'm a tramp, an obstacle keeping him from sleeping with Dr. Yee, his psychotherapist. According to Ray I'm preventing him from talking to strangers when in fact he is terrifying them with his uncontrollable babbling, and annoying them as he reeks of alcohol. On the way to Sedona he said I'm keeping him from being free, free like the way Brixton and Buddy run in the fenced city dog parks back home. He insists he can fly, if I let him go.

When another half hour passes and Ray still hasn't returned to the parking garage where he ran off, I go to our hotel. We are staying at the El Portal, the fanciest dog hotel in Sedona, known for welcoming pets with their own pet patio. The plastered adobe walls are eighteen inches thick, with cool Saltillo tiles on the floor, and the old Wild West antiques decorated in the California arts and crafts style. The buzzing of the cicada swarms is deafening in the heat, and I close the door, turning on the ceiling fan. Exhausted, I relish the silence, and in the bathroom the antique claw-foot tub looks luxurious. I forget about passing Ray as the dogs and I drove past him. There was no shoulder to pull off the road, I reasoned to myself. I would've lost him again.

But Ray eventually finds his way home, slams the door, and hurls his gym bag onto the bed. He removes his shoes, and one of his socks is seeped in bloodstains, right over his ankle. He lifts up a pant cuff and pulls out a silver scabbard, with what appears to be a ten-inch blade.

"What the hell?" I ask. "What is that thing?"

"It's a weapon, what does it look like? Since you left, and I'm walking around in a strange place, I needed to protect myself. Now, will we get to see the Grand Canyon? I want to go NOW!" He places the sword gently on top of his gym bag but his eyes are ablaze with anger.

"Sure," I say, startled, answering the demon that suddenly entered my life. "No problem. First thing tomorrow. The park's closed."

"You lie!" he shrieks, and sticks both middle fingers up at me. "You are a bitch."

He collapses with a thud and sinks. I pretend to listen to some unintelligible demands and slowly I move away. Ten seconds later, silence. Despite the exhaustion after his walk through town, his sleep will be a disturbing one filled with shaky leg syndrome, twitching, and other alcohol-induced tremors. He will remember none of this.

I call Michelle, Buddy's new mom, and tell her my location. Ahead of schedule, I took I-60 at the Texas border, and from Clovis I drove west, bypassing Michelle and touring through New Mexico, figuring we'd see Arizona and the Grand Canyon first, then double back toward Albuquerque. I tell her about the trip, the scene with the knife, and I hear the worry in her voice. There is a pause and then my friend's voice is calm again and I scribble down an address and a phone number—the number of a rehab place she says I can call once we get to Albuquerque.

"It's off Wyoming and Menaul Boulevard. Not too far from me," she says. "You're making great time, you know, four days . . . wow. No rush. But just get there, to Menaul. Tomorrow morning."

She tells me she no longer rushes anywhere, period, and I envy her terribly. I hang up and then call the number she gave me, and ask to speak to a guy named Fredo.

I tell him about my travels with my demon, who's now snoring and twitching. I throw out medical jargon I've heard, like co-morbidity, bipolar diagnosis, elevated enzyme levels. Mild schizophrenia and medications to treat these maladies were suggested by a therapist back home, but the condition now has worsened. I start to ramble on and I get the sense Fredo's heard this all before, because three-quarters of the way into my phone call he interrupts me and urges us to come in tomorrow, as opposed to New Mexico General, two miles away.

"The ER, well, this is the sixth poorest state in the nation," he says. "You take him there, and it'll probably kill him."

5. NE Albuquerque, New Mexico

Ray sleeps in the car as I speed from Sedona to the New Mexico border. When he stirs, I lie, and tell him we're making a liquor stop before seeing the wonders of the Grand Canyon. He lies in a fetal position, his legs atop Buddy's, and says this is the worst he has ever felt, and I know there isn't much time left before his sleep will wear off and painful cravings begin. It is late morning, and I put the Jeep in overdrive.

We are 6,000 feet above sea level when I reach Albuquerque. Reminds me of Van Nuys and most of the San Fernando Valley of Southern California, but without smog and palm trees. We drive past miles of strip malls and used furniture stores, most of their facades covered with fading signs. I am at home with streets like these that are three lanes wide in one direction, and I wonder how I managed to stay in NYC for so long. I make a note to try a local fast food restaurant named Blake's Lotaburgers. Their signs across town tell me to "Relax! Nutella shakes are here," and now I am thirsty.

I turn up Menaul Boulevard Northeast, past Lovelace Medical Center, then turn into a strip mall entrance with parking dividers mulched with white pebbles. The detox center is here, and I leave the car's AC running so the dogs can tolerate the midday heat.

"Is Fredo here?" I ask the receptionist. She looks at my disheveled and disoriented husband, apparently sizing him up to determine the strength of the orderly necessary should there be any resistance. She looks at me with a tight smile, and presses a buzzer to let us in the waiting area. Ray turns to me.

"I think I need to talk to a priest first," he says. "I know I'm sick but I'm scared. I think I'm possessed!"

"You know this is what you need to do, it'll be all right. You have to trust me on this."

Fredo enters, a slim man in his early thirties, wearing small tribal earrings, and younger than I imagined. Speaking with a slight lisp, he greets us, hands Ray a cup, and waits by the restroom door.

"Is this where you leave me?" Ray asks when he returns. We are both tired. I feel awful. I didn't think it would be this bad.

"For a very short while," I say. "I'll get your things."

He has not brought any camera equipment on this roadtrip. His blue gym bag contains a day's change of clothes, a quart of Georgi vodka, and a magazine. I think the knife is underneath the dog bed, back in the Arizona hotel room.

I walk past a large man wearing a clean fitted polo shirt, casually standing by the entrance door. He's a staff member, doubling as security. I see him, but he's trying to be invisible, holding up a newspaper to cover his face. I am not too far from the dog park where I'm supposed to meet Michelle. Chile roasting season—I can smell it in the September air. I drive out of the lot, knowing I should head for the dog park, but instead I take a deep breath and turn left, in search of one of those Nutella milkshakes.

Agatha Z. Roa is a feminist writer, traveler, and community gardener/food justice activist. She is a VONA (Voices of Our Nation Arts Foundation) fellow, a Hedgebrook/VORTEXT alum, and a former student of author Frank McCourt. She has written for urbangardensweb.com as well as the *Mini-Press*, a trade advocacy newspaper for the NYC Taxi and Limousine Commission. Formerly working in advertising and public affairs, she now plans to pursue her MFA in fiction, blogs at vinebarkandpour.com, and keeps a virtual log of her gardening pursuits on her Twitter feed @BrooklynBlooms.

He's Sober Today

Sheryl L. Nelms

no money
to pay the car insurance

or the truck
payment

or the rent
or the gas bill
electricity bill
phone bill
AOL
or Dish satellite

it is coming
five thousand dollars

but we don't
know
when

or if it
will
be

soon
enough

but he is
sober

today

Sheryl L. Nelms is from Marysville, Kansas, and graduated from South Dakota State University. She has published over 5,000 articles, stories, and poems, including fourteen collections of poetry, and is a three-time Pushcart Prize nominee. More information on her credits can be found at www.pw.org/directory/featured. Sheryl's personal connection to recovery comes through her husband, who drank for forty one years. Seven years ago he went to an alcohol and drug rehab center through an intervention and has been sober since then. Every year Sheryl and her husband go to the rehab center's annual reunion with joy in their hearts and a prayer of thanks for these last seven years.

THE CONNECTION

Introduction to The Connection

The intense, authentic desire of people in recovery to help those who, as poet Shane Crady says in "The Gift I See," are "still lost in the dark" of addiction is immense and palpable in the pages that follow.

Many people in recovery answer the call to attend the suffering, as Jesus does in "The Lost Gospel" by Jim Littwin. Some of us are simple deliverers of soup, as in Elizabeth Brulé Farrell's poem, "Out of the Hospital." That's important too.

Or, like Aaron Holst in "Shooting Star or Beacon?," we drive long highway miles to deliver a suffering comrade to the safety of treatment, just because we heard the crucial words: *Will you take me?*

Sometimes we see someone lost in their addiction and have a *There, but for the grace of God* moment, as in Tom Larsen's "Ghost Story."

Sometimes we feel the need to thank a person who helped us find a way to gain recovery without losing our essential selves, the way Billi Johnson-Casey does in "Thanking Anne Lamott."

Recovery Community Organizations, like Recover Wyoming, play an important matchmaking role. Through programs like peer-to-peer mentoring and recovery coaching, people seeking recovery are linked with people in long-term recovery. The connection is magical. The mentor/coach points the way: *Exit from addiction HERE*, and at the same time gets a vital reminder about the tools necessary to maintain their own recovery.

Lost Gospel

Jim Littwin

And at that time
Jesus broke away from us
and waded into weeds,
plastic bags,
and broken glass
under a billboard
and knelt beside
a drunken man
curled and cursing,
shivering in his own sickness.

There in the dirt
Jesus sat him up
and said words to him
we couldn't hear,
for we wouldn't go near.

And the man did not
stop drinking immediately
thereafter, but followed us
at a distance,
from that day.

And sometimes,
Jesus would wave us away
and turn to walk with that man,
to ask him questions,
then listen and listen.

Jim Littwin's poems and stories have appeared in *The National Catholic Reporter, Story Quarterly, Whetstone, Hyphen Magazine, Willow Review, The Daily Herald, Saint Anthony Messenger, The Grapevine*, and other publications. A retired teacher who lives in Chicago, he is a good friend of Bill W. and Dr. Bob.

Since Leticia Williams Saw Jesus

Patty Somlo

Leticia Williams shook hands with Jesus on her very last day of rehab. The handshake occurred an hour before group and moments after she'd finished combing her hair. She had taken an extra minute to admire her reflection in the mirror, pleased at how her cheeks had filled out and her eyes had cleared. She had large, dark brown eyes, cocoa-colored skin, and a long, thin face. Her hair was straightened and neatly combed. The high cheekbones drew attention to her eyes.

About to turn around and take a last look to make sure she'd packed up all her things, Leticia Williams saw Jesus, standing behind her reflection in the far right-hand corner of the mirror.

The breath left her, almost as if she'd been punched in the stomach. She feared those crazy damned hallucinations she'd had in detox were coming back. The only thing to do was turn around.

Her back to the mirror, Leticia saw the wavy brown hair and the off-white robe she'd just seen reflected.

"You real, ain't ya?" Leticia asked.

Jesus silently reached out his right hand.

"You Jesus," Leticia exhaled the words, her heart rattling in her chest and her throat gone dry.

He smiled and nodded, his clean brown hair reflecting the light. Leticia could only stare.

"Oh," Leticia said. "You waitin' on me, ain't ya?"

Leticia stepped toward the man, her legs shaking. She reached her trembling hand out, sure that when she tried to touch Jesus' hand, he would exist only in her mind. She curled her fingers. The warmth of Jesus' flesh was all the proof she needed.

"You real," she said.

A smile edged out from the corner of Jesus' lips as he shook Leticia's hand.

The next moment, Jesus was gone. Leticia pulled her hand back and studied it. She wondered what in heaven's name she ought to do now. Still staring at her hand, Leticia wondered, *What is a woman supposed to do after she has shaken Jesus' hand*?

At first, Leticia was hesitant to tell a single soul, knowing how easy it could be to confuse a vision with one of those hallucinations. But after graduation, in the cafeteria, its walls hung with red and blue crepe paper, and colored balloons strung down from the ceiling, and everyone standing around in their best dresses and a couple of guys in suits, with little kids running around screaming, Leticia thought about the moment she'd shared with Jesus and smiled.

"What you glowin' for, Leticia Williams?"

Diane Larson was standing a little too close for Leticia's comfort. Leticia took a couple of steps back as she gave Diane the once-over. Diane was wearing a white clingy dress, one the girl had probably worn when she was out hustling on the street. There was too much skin exposed at the top and bottom of the dress to be decent.

"I'm just happy." Leticia took a sip of fruit punch, thinking for the umpteenth time since getting out of bed that she hadn't had a drink in seven months.

"Kind of strange to be happy and not be usin', huh?" Diane asked.

Leticia considered the question. It bothered her that Diane talked like she was black.

"They's other stuff to be glad about," Leticia said.

"Yeah. Like movin' to our own apartments."

Without planning to, Leticia said, "I had a visitor today." She let out what had happened when she was getting dressed for graduation.

Word spread that Leticia Williams had shaken hands with Jesus. It drifted around amongst the folks who'd made it all the way through the program. Then it seeped into stories shared by men and women still struggling to control the demons of drugs and drink. People standing outside the clinic smoking—before and after group—and the ones on methadone who'd come for their daily dosing shared the news.

Marleena Wright was the first to ask Leticia for a meeting. She'd relapsed over the weekend and her counselor threatened that one more time and Marleena would lose her apartment.

"I was wondering," Marleena said to Leticia as they streamed out of the office filled with old sagging couches, where their group met. Marleena caught a piece of Leticia's red satin blouse in her fingers, which made Leticia mad.

"What was you wonderin'?" Leticia asked, as soon as they got outside and moved away from the group congregating in front of the clinic.

Marleena's shoulder-length hair had been bleached so many times, it looked like the woman had left it outside on a sizzling afternoon in July. The roots were growing back, black and hard. Leticia was tempted to ask Marleena if she had any idea what she looked like.

Marleena pulled a cigarette out of her bag, pressed her lips around the filter, and lit the end with a green plastic lighter.

"I ain't got all day, Marleena. You wanna tell me what you was wonderin'?"

"I was wonderin' if maybe I could come talk to you," Marleena said. "Sometime soon. Everybody's been saying that since you saw Jesus, you have some special healing powers. If I slide back one more time, that might be it for me."

Minutes before Marleena arrived, Leticia lit seven candles and set them on the coffee table and the little TV trays she used as side tables in the one-room apartment. She turned on one lamp next to the bed. She wasn't sure how a woman might go about becoming a healer. But she'd been in and out of rehab so many times, talking to this and that counselor, it was easy to move over to the helping side.

"Oooh," was all Marleena said when she stepped inside.

Leticia told Marleena to sit down in one of the two metal chairs at the little table where she ate. She gave Marleena a cup of jasmine tea.

"So." Leticia sat down at the table across from Marleena. "What d'ya want to know?"

Marleena picked at the chipped dark purple polish on her index fingernail. She was shaking some, the way people did in group when they were still using. Marleena raised her head from studying her fingers and Leticia could see that the woman looked about to bawl.

"I . . . I, well, I just thought. I mean, I wondered. I mean, if you saw Jesus, well, then maybe you could teach me how."

Marleena went back to messing with her fingernails.

Leticia wasn't sure how to respond. She didn't have a clue why Jesus had unexpectedly decided to show up in her life. And it wasn't like she had any kind of special connection, like she could just call Jesus up on the phone and say, "Hey look, Jesus. I got this friend Marleena, and she be needin' you right now."

But Leticia could see that Marleena needed help to keep from sliding back into a life of using and hustling, a world she'd get lost in, until most of her teeth were gone and her cheeks had sunk in, and she'd end up in jail, with half her mind gone.

"Let us pray on it a minute," she said.

Leticia stretched both arms out on the table. Marleena stopped fussing with her nails and clasped each of Leticia's hands. Their hands, dark and light with the fingers entwined, made a nice pattern on the scratched fake-wood table. Leticia took a deep breath and closed her eyes.

Leticia wasn't sure what to be praying for. She was distracted by the shaking coming from Marleena's fingers.

But then a picture came into Leticia's mind of Marleena standing on the sidewalk next to the liquor store. Leticia had seen her there when Marleena was still using, in those high sandals that looked like blocks under her feet and that bleached hair looking like the wind had just messed with it. Leticia remembered the sadness on Marleena's face, even though those red-painted lips of hers were smiling.

That's when Leticia asked Jesus if he might possibly come back. She explained to him that she wasn't asking for herself. "You see, Jesus," Leticia silently pleaded—she didn't want Marleena to know that Leticia couldn't bring Jesus into the room whenever she wanted—"this girl, Marleena, she needs you, Jesus. If you show up, that might be all it takes."

A moment later, Leticia was startled when Marleena shouted, "Oh, my." Leticia opened her eyes.

"What is it?" Leticia asked.

"It's him." Marleena's wide-open eyes were looking somewhere behind Leticia's head. Her hands loosened from Leticia's grip.

"What d'ya see?" Leticia asked.

Marleena started to cry.

"D'ya see somethin'?"

"Yes." Marleena ran a finger under her dripping nose. Her fingers were shaking. "Jesus," she whispered, so soft that Leticia had to lean in close. "Jesus. He's right there."

Leticia wondered if she ought to turn around and make sure Jesus was standing there. She started to swivel at the waist, but then she changed her mind.

"You might ask him to help you," Leticia whispered back. "Ask him to help you stay straight."

One by one, the women from the program and then a handful of men came to see Leticia. On each visit, Leticia lit seven candles and turned off all the lights, except the one small lamp next to the bed. And every one of the people who came to Leticia seeking help had a moment, after holding Leticia's hands while she prayed, when Jesus appeared.

Leticia continued to keep her back to Jesus. She thought about it sometimes when she was alone, blowing out the candles, the apartment dark and smoky. What if she turned around one evening and Jesus was gone?

Since the morning she had shaken his hand, Leticia herself hadn't had a glimpse of Jesus. But she'd also been blessed. Not a single one of those crazy hallucinations had occurred.

Of course, the clean and sober life was not always easy. Every time Leticia made a mistake in school—leaving the straightening solution on too long so the hair got brittle, or getting the razor too close to the skin and causing the client to bleed—she had to clamp her jaw tight and grind her teeth to keep from screaming. There'd been incidents too, when Leticia had thrown the scissors and comb on the floor and stomped away and Andre, her teacher, needed to sit with her while she had a minor breakdown.

Jesus was nowhere to be found the night Leticia Williams relapsed. It was a man—a pure flesh and blood man—who was the cause. His name was Rodney and he had skin the color of hot fudge on a sundae, before it mixes with the vanilla ice cream. He called Leticia "baby, baby" when they made love, and told her she had the most *be-u-tiful* eyes.

And then Leticia saw Rodney with his lips on Diane Larson's neck and his hands running all over her body. He ground Diane's ass into his groin and then started to sway, like they were dancing.

Leticia marched right over to him on the sidewalk outside the clinic.

"What you doin' with that whore?" Leticia screamed at Rodney, standing practically on top of him. Rodney looked up, still hanging onto Diane Larson.

"Ain't no business of yours," Rodney said.

"It sure is my business." Leticia grabbed him by the arm.

"Get your hands offa me." Rodney shoved Leticia back. "Get away from me, bitch."

Jesus did not accompany Leticia when she sprinted straight over from the clinic to the liquor store. He did not sit with her as she gulped herself into a stupor. And the next morning, when she slept in, missing class at the beauty school, Jesus didn't bother to try and wake her.

In fact, that entire week, when Leticia barely ate and guzzled one bottle of thick, sweet red wine after another, Jesus didn't stop by. Leticia ignored the phone when it rang, so she couldn't be certain that Jesus hadn't called.

It was Marleena who got the landlord to open the apartment door. And it was Marleena who lowered Leticia into the tub and washed her hair and face, her legs and arms, and helped her into some clean clothes. Marleena fed Leticia spoonfuls of chicken noodle soup and went with her the next morning to group. Marleena even stayed over a couple of nights, curled up on the couch, to make sure Leticia didn't go out and buy more wine.

One warm July evening, several weeks later, Marleena lit seven candles and turned off the lights. She stretched her arms across the fake-wood table in Leticia's apartment and waited for Leticia to grab her hands. Then she closed her eyes and prayed for Jesus to come to Leticia's aid.

Leticia opened her eyes. She looked past Marleena's bleached blond hair. And then she waited, keeping her eyes fixed there.

The candles flickering in the room caused the shadows of the two women to tango across the wall. Leticia waited a little longer, but nothing remotely resembling Jesus popped up anywhere around.

Leticia studied her friend, who had her eyes closed, mumbling in prayer. She noticed that Marleena's fingers weren't shaking as they had been. Leticia thought about miracles and how belief could maybe make almost anything occur. And though she didn't see Jesus standing there, she went ahead and said, "Oh my goodness. I see him. He's here."

Patty Somlo has received four Pushcart Prize nominations, been nominated for the storySouth Million Writers Award and had an essay selected as a Notable Essay of 2013 *for Best American Essays 2014.* Author of *From Here to There and Other Stories* and the just-released short story collection, *The First to Disappear* (Spuyten Duyvil), Somlo has two forthcoming books: a memoir, *Even When Trapped Behind Clouds* (WiDo Publishing), and *Hairway to Heaven Stories* (Cherry Castle Publishing). Her work has appeared in journals, including the *Los Angeles Review, the Santa Clara Review, Under the Sun, Guernica, Gravel, Sheepshead Review,* and *WomenArts Quarterly,* and numerous anthologies. Find her at www.pattysomlo.com, on Amazon at http://www.amazon.com/Patty-Somlo/e/B006T340US, or follow on Twitter @PattySomlo.

Connoisseur

Rebecca Taksel

I will not write about single malt scotches,
I leave them to the deeply brooding British detectives
who can pronounce Laphroaig and
know the difference between Speyside and Skye.

I will not write about gin,
not even gin martinis straight up,
not even a certain gin martini, a gibson really—
those darling little onions on a stick—
served at the Pump Room in Chicago years ago.

I will most certainly not write about vodka,
which is just gin that doesn't smell,
the drink of cowards,
the drink whose only excuse was the beautiful Russian names:
Stolichnaya!
The Americans gave it a goddamned nickname.
Well, go ahead, drink your Stoly while you read Tony Chekhov.

I will not write about beer,
and even if I did write about it,
I would not, repeat not, write about light beer,
though capitalism has amply rewarded the genius
who convinced even outlaw motorcyclists
that it's okay to walk into a bar and say Bud Light.

The list is long:
The liqueurs with gorgeous names
like Chambord and Chartreuse,
and the one and only Mr. Daniels,
all-American descendant of the great European dynasty
which I can pronounce in French *and* Spanish.

I will, finally and emphatically, not write about wine:
No glass of chardonnay,
no big fat glass of a big fat merlot,
no glass of Château Margaux,
no Pétrus, no Saint-Emilion.
At the lower price points:
No glass of wine out of a box,
no glass of Mad-Dog 20/20.
That's no glass of wine, period, get it?

As the elegant lady at the meeting years ago reminded me,
"We never had *one* glass of wine in our lives!"
Right you are, lovely lady, and what's more,
the distance between Château Saint-Julien
and Boone's Farm
is the distance
between home and wherever the nearest liquor store is at closing time.
No thousand-dollar Bordeaux at the corner store? No problem.
The whole world obliges: Chile, Australia, Spain.
What the hell? Oregon, Ohio, New York.
Name your poison, honey,
just don't ask me to write about it.

I am, however, going to write, very briefly, here,
about a phone call I made, finally, late one night,
after I'd spent some hours
alone, sitting on a flat rock
listening to the waves on a beach
of the vast inland sea that touches Chicago
and heard my own voice escape
into the rush of wind and water,
calling for help,

And about how I learned, finally,
that the taste of pure water
fills my body and my mind with sunlight.

Rebecca Taksel lives in Pittsburgh, Pennsylvania. Her nonfiction appeared between 2004 and 2014 in *The Redwood Coast Review,* published in Mendocino County, California. She became a contributing editor of the *Review.* Her novel, *Come Away,* is on the spring 2016 list of Little Feather Books. Rebecca contributed articles to *Natural Home* magazine, which reflected her many years of experience in the interior design field. She also wrote reviews and articles for *Animals' Agenda,* which was for many years the only independent magazine of advocacy for animals. Her essays have appeared in anthologies about gardening and companion animals; she has also contributed personal essays to the *Pittsburgh Post-Gazette,* Pittsburgh's venerable daily newspaper.

Rebecca is a recovering alcoholic with twenty-nine years' sobriety thanks to Alcoholics Anonymous. Sobriety allowed her to pick up the threads of creativity and productivity that had unraveled during long years of addiction. Until her recent retirement, Rebecca worked in Pittsburgh as a French and English teacher at the college level, and she had her own business buying and selling antique books and textiles. She continues to consult in interior design for her sister's firm in Chicago. She credits the spirit of the Serenity Prayer and the AA philosophy of "One day at a time" for making this stage of her long life the happiest, most useful, and most creative.

The Gift I See

Shane Ronel Crady

Sometimes it's hard to see the **good in people**
when they're hauling you off to jail. But now that
I've been free from the control of addiction, **one
thing I know with certainty** is I was trapped in a **wasteland**
that caused an ugly wound. Now **the gift I see** is
I'm no longer out there in the **dark freezing night** searching
for just one more. I'm beginning to feel **a great power**
from within myself. I don't know why
but I feel the need to light a **candle**
I think it's my way of saying a **prayer**
for those still lost in the dark.
May they find their way in the night.

Shane Ronel Crady is a poet who lives in Lawrence, Kansas, and was a participant in Brian Daldorph's writing class.

Shane says, "I write a lot and it's all dark but it's all very real. I've lived a life outside the box and addiction has led the way, not necessarily drugs but money and running the streets and feeding off the addiction of others. Karma put me right there with them and addicted just the same. My goal is to help people find freedom from their addiction and maybe help others realize they don't want to travel that road to begin with."

Thanking Anne Lamott

Billi Johnson-Casey

"Shit or get off the pot!"

I knew that my daughter was right. I had almost forgotten that she and her husband were in the front seat as I sat in the back trying to slow my racing heart. My daughter made it clear that if we were going in, we needed to do it now. I could only imagine what my son-in-law was thinking.

Time was running out and so was patience in the front seat. I'd been planning and picturing this for months. I was visiting California for a week and would be returning to Illinois soon. This was a now or never situation. There was a part of me that had believed all along that, even if we got here, the church or the woman wouldn't be real. But I was looking at St. Andrew Presbyterian Church. It was real. So was the green Subaru that pulled in and parked next to us and so was the woman who emerged from that Subaru. There was no mistaking those blond dreadlocks—Anne Lamott had just arrived.

Seven years before I'd sat in a different parking lot, one that was, literally and figuratively, thousands of miles away from where I was now. As police cars screeched into that parking lot and blocked me in, I knew I'd been caught. Unexpected relief washed over me and I thought, *Maybe this is the thing that will keep me from killing myself.* It's not like there hadn't been other events and circumstances prior to that which should have put a stop to my drug use, but so far . . . nothing had. I'd started drinking and using at fifteen and had continued for the next twenty-seven years despite the countless negative consequences. And then, there

I was, getting arrested for calling in a prescription for Vicodin. I'd like to say that starting at that moment a light went on, a switch flipped, and I never touched another drug, but that wouldn't be true. It took me another five months, a nearly fatal overdose, and being put on probation before I would, for the first time in my adult life, spend eighteen months free of any drugs or alcohol.

As part of my probation I'd been ordered to attend twelve-step meetings, have the leader of each meeting sign a paper proving that I'd attended, and bring the paper to my probation officer once a month. The people in the meetings went out of their way to make me feel welcome and I saw that their program worked for them; however, I wasn't convinced that it was going to work for me. Knowing that I needed something more, I turned to a thing that had, so often throughout my life, offered me entertainment and escape as well as answers: books. I read everything I could get my hands on that was written by or for addicts.

One Friday night when I had three or four months clean, I left a meeting feeling restless and unnerved. I had gotten through the worst of the physical part of getting clean, but now I was being forced to live without the one thing that I believed made life possible for me to deal with. The one thing that made me a fun, interesting person. The one thing, other than my children, that I couldn't imagine living the rest of my life without. Not ready to go home, I went to Barnes & Noble instead. On the outside, I looked fine, but my brain felt like Bambi on that frozen pond. Thumper might be laughing, but I wasn't. I headed directly to the shelves of books on addiction. As my eyes scanned the books, my brain ticked off: *I've read that one, I've read that one, I've read that one.* I started to panic. *How could I have read all of these books and still not found an answer? What if I read everything there was to read and I still didn't have this shit figured out?* Just as I reached a point where I either needed to find a book I hadn't read or find a paper bag to breathe into, a title caught my eye. *The Harder They Fall: Celebrities Tell Their Real-Life Stories of Addiction and Recovery.*

I snatched it off the shelf and read the back cover: Alice Cooper, Steve Earle, Mariette Hartley, Richard Lewis, Malachy McCourt, Chuck Negron, Richard Prior, and Grace Slick were among the people whose stories were included inside. Alice Cooper and Grace Slick and Richard

Pryor—oh my! It didn't get any cooler than that. I bought the book and cracked it open as soon as I got home. I started with the essays by the people I was familiar with, and then proceeded on to the essays by people I hadn't heard of. All the stories had different characters, different settings, different details—yet the journeys were the same. Each one was inspiring and spoke to me, at least on an intellectual level.

I finished reading about Dock Ellis at around two in the morning. One side effect of removing opiates from your system is a difficulty in being able to sleep. I was finally tired, but as I put the book down, the page turned and there, with fabulous blond dreads and eyes of pure understanding, was Anne Lamott. It looked like an essay I'd like to read at some point, but not tonight. Then the William Cowper quote that she'd chosen for the beginning of her piece caught my eye:

> The clouds ye so much dread
> Are big with mercy and shall break
> In blessings on your head.

The.clouds.ye.so.much.dread.are.big.with.mercy.and.shall.break.in.blessings.on.your.head.

I read it. Over and over. And I wept. It was the first time since getting clean that words had made their way around my brain and into my gut. I was TERRIFIED of what the clouds of a future without an anesthetized brain held for me.

I am not a person who romanticizes events. I believe in coincidence, but not fate. I don't believe that everything happens for a reason. But in that moment, I believed that Anne Lamott had left me a note—much like a note from a mother sent in a lunch box on the first day of school—an assurance that I could do this. And for the first time, I believed it.

My son-in-law had opted to sleep in the car during the service, but my daughter and I made our way into the church and found seats on the far right side. Anne sat in the section that mirrored ours. Had the sanctuary been a scale, she would have been my counterbalance. Partway through the service Anne left with a few teenagers. I knew from reading her essays that she taught Sunday school classes and assumed that's where they were headed. I held a card on which I'd written the things I needed to tell her and planned to leave it with someone if I didn't get the chance to meet Anne. I also brought a copy of her book, *Bird By Bird*, for her to sign and a camera so I could have a picture of myself with her. There was nothing to do now but sit back and wait, politely, while the pastor gave the sermon. I anticipated a sermon that would be full of Jesusy things that I, as an atheist, wouldn't agree with and didn't want to hear. It remains a mystery to me why I doubted that I would find inspiration and wisdom from a source where Anne had clearly gained so much of her own. As I listened to the sermon, I was moved by words that were, like the "clouds ye so much dread" quote, not written by Anne, but words that she was responsible for my having heard. I didn't doubt that the universe knew I was coming and knew what I needed to hear.

"Although we had lost contact, my brother and I were once close," the minister was saying. "I was at a culinary store that is a couple hours from my home. An employee was demonstrating a cooking technique using salt blocks. I remembered that my brother fancied himself an amateur chef and thought it would be a great gift for him."

She went on to talk about how, even though she thought about sending the salt block to her brother, she didn't do it because they didn't have much of a relationship anymore. She returned home, but couldn't get the salt block or her brother out of her head. A few days later she made the two-hour drive back to the store, bought the salt block, and shipped it to her brother.

"He called to thank me and we ended up spending several hours on the phone: laughing, crying, apologizing, and forgiving. That was five years ago and we have rebuilt our relationship. I almost didn't send that salt block. I learned that day that if there's something that you feel the need to do for someone, by all means, you should. Don't let yourself 'think' away the 'feel' of it."

I'd had doubts about making this trip from the first time the idea went through my mind, up until this moment. Sometimes it felt like a divine mission, other times it felt stalkerish. However, during the sermon, any doubt I'd had about my quest to thank Anne Lamott disappeared. Even if she ran away screaming, I needed to see this through. After the service, I approached one of the women who'd gotten up and spoken and was clearly also a recovering addict. I explained that Anne Lamott's words had probably saved my life and had definitely saved my sanity.

"I have this card for her," I said, as my courage and resolve began to flounder. "Could you give it to her, please?"

"No," said the woman with a facial expression that gave nothing away. "You need to give it to her yourself." With that she turned and walked out the sanctuary door and into the courtyard. My daughter and I followed.

After finding Anne's essay that night, and being rocked by the quote she'd selected, it had taken me a few days to pick the book back up. At the time, I didn't know what my hesitation was, but looking back, I think I feared answers as strongly as I craved them.

It was not going to be easy. I'd been lying to everyone for my entire life. What she showed me through her truth was that the person I'd lied to the most was myself. Being radically honest with myself would be my salvation. It was, and always will be, the biggest factor when it comes to keeping myself from going down the path of self-destruction, no matter whether that path is paved with drugs or men or self-centeredness or any of the other things I'm capable of using to run my life into the gutter.

The churchgoer who had decided not to be my personal US Postal Service led us across the courtyard and into a small room where the Sunday school class was wrapping up. Everyone in the room, Anne included, stopped what they were doing and stared at us. Fortunately, our guide gave a brief synopsis of what was going on. I was at a loss for words.

How do you thank a woman who, without any knowledge of it, went from being a stranger to a savior?

How do you thank her for finding the way, sharing her story, and in doing so convincing you that life could be a thousand times better without drugs?

How do you thank her for leading you and your estranged daughter back to each other?

How do you thank her for writing the words that provided a light at the end of a dark, hopeless tunnel and inspiring you to do the same for others?

You just do.

I don't remember exactly what I said to Anne or all of what she said to me. I do remember her introducing me to a couple who was in the room.

"This is Barb and Kevin. They're like us. Crazy as shit."

Who says that?

Someone who is fabulous and nutty and maybe a little awkward in the wake of a grateful stranger showing up to thank her. Someone who is going to be just fine with the fact that she didn't, in that moment, have something profound or eloquent to say. Someone who taught me that it's okay for me to be imperfectly myself, too.

I made the decision to leave my camera and my copy of *Bird By Bird* in my purse. I don't have a picture with her or an autographed copy of her book, but it didn't feel right to ask for either. I was there to say thank you, not to ask for more than she'd already given me.

As we were saying our good-byes, Anne mentioned that she'd recently celebrated the anniversary of her clean date. I knew that she started her journey many years before I did. What I didn't know until that moment was that both of us celebrated the anniversary of that beginning every year on July 7th.

After a "misunderstanding" with the law nine years ago Billi Johnson-Casey ended a twenty-five year, losing battle with drugs. In what may have been a midlife crisis, she left a career as an RN and returned to school to pursue a degree in publishing studies and literature. She does stand-up comedy and has had the pleasure of working with some fabulous people including Bobcat Goldthwait, Maria Bamford, Charlie Murphy and many others. She's had essays published in *Bluffs Literary Magazine* and works as a writing consultant at Illinois Central College.

Out of the Hospital

Elizabeth Brulé Farrell

The first week home he wrangled
with pain on his couch. The voices
of characters on t.v. his companions.
On the other side of the stucco wall
my voice shouted as I stood with soup
to soothe the pancreatitis, the inflamed liver,
my elixir to his near alcoholic death.

I had to wait for his body to rise,
do its slow shuffle to turn the lock.
His face a startling canvas of despair,
he took the soup and shut the door.

The next week I brought a roast chicken.
He stood against the door and smiled.
No words exchanged between us, but
the window shades were pulled up,
the empty bottles with their sticky liquid
were gone. His hand did not shake
when he took mine into his.

Shooting Star or Beacon?

Aaron E. Holst

Rodeo Saturday brings crowds to downtown Sheridan, Wyoming, for the annual dance. It's a time when bars can serve past 2:00 a.m., the street is closed to traffic, and roundups for the "all-night rodeo" begin. If a road could suffer a hangover, you can see it on Main on Rodeo Sunday.

Red stoplights blink as if trying to clear bloodshot eyes. Beer cups and trash hug the ground. Clusters of portable toilets line the sidewalks, wait for someone to take them home. Unused ice melts into the street from powerless coolers that look like passed-out drunks in the gutters peeing their pants. Stale beer and puke perfume the air, garbage cans gag.

My summer exercise routine includes bicycling through the town. When my bike rolls along Main Street on Rodeo Sunday mornings, I marvel that my body does not feel the way this street looks. My head and eyes are clear and free of pain. My stomach is at peace with its contents, and my spirit, unencumbered by guilt or shame. The emotional and physical relief I feel radiates into my legs and feet and I drive the bike's pedals with strong, steady turns into another day free from alcohol.

Overwhelming desperation led to the beginning of my recovery—April 29, 1984, too drunk to stand, crawling the floor with the insane thought that if I drank more, the euphoria would finally return, even though it hadn't in years. Hopeless, helpless, wanting to die, I finally called a friend who would help.

He asked, "Are you willing to go to any length to quit drinking?"

"Yes."

"I know two ways to do this, AA or treatment."

"What's the difference?" I asked.

"Treatment is a head-start to quitting."

Thinking how special I considered myself, that I deserved head-starts, I chose treatment.

"If I can get you in today, will you go?"

"Yes."

"How will you get there?"

"I don't know."

"I'll see if my dad can take you."

Several terrifying hours later—*terrifying* because I feared I would once again convince myself that my drinking really wasn't *that* bad—my friend's dad and I were finally on the road to a center in Montana where my twenty-eight-day stay included misery and joy, relief and shame, release and fear.

Near the end of treatment, a counselor led us through a values clarification activity that involved choices between two options. At one point, she asked, "Do you see yourself as a shooting star or a beacon?" I chose and clearly recall why. A shooting star flashes across the sky quickly, burning intensely and, I reasoned, momentarily. A beacon stands solid, its beam steady, brilliant, uninterrupted. My selection: beacon.

So how does this choice relate to my recovery? Two concrete examples stand out, both tied to helping others.

A friend of mine suffered as did I and my fear grew that he would not make the call, might face death from his drinking. It took an event that ends all too often in tragedy: a raging drunk confronted by a young son with a loaded pistol protecting a threatened family. Fortunately, the police arrived in time to intervene and removed my friend from his home.

After his release in the early morning hours, he called. "How much gas is in your car?"

I could tell he had been drinking, was probably still drunk. "Why?"

"I want you to take me to treatment."

"Where are you?"

"At my dad's house."

As I drove to his father's home, I wrestled with what to say, what to do. Then, I remembered my own experience. "If you can get in today will you go?"

"Yes. Will you take me?"

"I will."

It was that simple. I made the contacts and, within hours we, too, were on the road. On the way, my friend related the reason for his call. After my return from treatment, he had intently watched my behavior, saw my commitment to sobriety, and knew I would help if asked. Honored by his call, humbled by his trust in me, it was then I realized how bright my beacon shone.

Another early-morning call, my youngest brother on the line with the latest: "Last night, Dad told Mom he had loaded his pistol with two bullets, one for her, one for him. Not sure what to do."

I paused, stunned by the news, unsure of what to say. Fear, anger, and hurt passed through the line between us until I reconnected with what I know, what I suspect, and what we can do.

"If he is in a blackout, he may not know he made this threat, could even carry it out without knowing. If we don't act quickly, someone might die."

We talked about intervention, what it is, what it means. We researched treatment resources in his community and identified those who would help in this process. Over the phone, I readied my brother for his role.

"The intervention will be uncomfortable. You will feel you are betraying our dad. But remember, it is a life and death matter and you must have the strength to carry this out. I know you can do it. Remember, too, the potential consequences of not intervening will be much more painful. If you need or want to talk, you can call me anytime, day or night."

You could use "pins and needles" to describe my wait for the next call, but those sensations won't come close—more like a head-swirling gut-churn through distracted days of listening for the phone until finally hearing my brother's voice: "It's done; he's going."

The heady relief of a successful intervention pulled my brother and me closer and I count him one of my heroes. "You did a wonderful, courageous thing today, probably saved their lives. I'm proud of you!"

I soon boarded a plane to participate in Dad's Family Day in treatment and celebrated another milestone: it was my first time to fly clean and sober.

Again, I felt honored by the call, grateful for my knowledge and experience, humbled to be part of Dad's recovery, and awed that the beam could reach from Wyoming to California. He and I were given the opportunity to repair our lives together, and, although he passed on in 2010, we shared many years of sobriety.

My recovery continues one day at a time, sometimes one hour at a time, occasionally one minute at a time. It includes participation in a recovery support group, daily acknowledgment that my life and sobriety rely on a Power greater than I, a commitment to help other alcoholics who still suffer, and the frequent reminder that my attitude and behavior transmit more than I can imagine.

Reference

Paul Hostovsky

I have worked as apprentice of sorts
to the wino in the park
for years. I keep an eye on his bottle of port
when he leaves it to piss in the pachysandra.

My predecessor struck out on his own
for the park across town
where he finally drowned in his own self pity.
So much for ambition.

Once, when I spoke of quitting, my employer
wept. He kissed me and praised
my perfect attendance. He offered to serve
as a reference.

The problem was his job title: the drunk.
And his address: the drunk in the park.
The drunk in the park is in.
What are the prospects

for someone bearing such a reference?
And where is the prospective employer
who will take it for what
it's worth?

Ghost Story

Tom Larsen

Angelo's may not be the best pizza in town, but at a buck a slice it keeps the locals connected. I'm on my way in when I see Joey G. coming out. I try to dodge him but forget about it.

"Hey, Rile, how you doing?"

"Good, Joey, I'm doing good."

"Christ, I haven't seen you since they sent up Hobbsy."

"Three years now. His mom just passed."

Marshall Hobbs, my former partner, presently serving zip/six at Graterford. For some stupid reason I think of Marshall when I shave every morning, always along the jawline, a flicker in my brain. I don't know what it means except those are good years going down the drain and somebody should feel bad about it.

"Me and Franny got a place on Fifty-Eighth," Joey tells me. "Nice place, two bedroom, we've been getting our shit together."

"Glad to hear it," I say what you say. Never mind Joey looks like hell and he and Fran have been getting their shit together for thirty years.

"Listen, Riley," he pulls me from the doorway. "I hate to ask you, man, but could you spot me a few bucks until my check comes?"

"Come on, Joey. I can't give you money to cop."

"It ain't like that. Franny's been sick. I can get it back to you in a couple of days."

I look him up and down. "Have you seen yourself lately? Your nose is running and your pupils are like manhole covers. What are you doing, Joey, everything?"

"Just this once, Riley, help me out."

"What about Fran? Is she as strung out as you?"

Joey's face goes hard. "Forget it, okay? Sorry I asked. Don't worry about me and Franny. We'll get along. I'll see you around, man." He pushes past me.

"Joey, hey!" I follow him outside. "Don't take it that way. It's just hard seeing you like this, man."

He pulls up, glassy eyed. "Franny's finished, Riley. Full blown, you wouldn't even recognize her."

" . . . I didn't know."

"Me and Fran?" His eyes go dead. "We don't belong in this world no more."

"Where is Franny? Is she in the hospital?"

"She's at home. They were gonna stick her in hospice, but she wants to die in her own bed." Joey's crying now and people give us lots of room.

"Look, I'm sorry, Joey. I wouldna said what I said if I knew about Fran. You know that, right?"

"Don't feel sorry for me, Riley. I couldn't take it."

"Can I see her? Would that be okay?"

"It's hard, man. I do the best I can." He chokes back a sob. "Remember, Riley, how she filled out that Maria Goretti uniform? Christ, I see it like it was yesterday."

I take his arm, just a stick through the thermal jacket. Their place isn't far and I brace myself, ten hard years since I last laid eyes. I know this house, the only one with a shotgun blast above the window, thank you DEA. I can smell Franny's sickness at the front door. The house is dark and quiet as a tomb.

"I better check first. Make sure she's up to it."

Joey ducks down the hall and I settle on the stairs. The walls going up are covered in photographs, black and whites from Franny's *Daily News* days. She was a dynamo back then, cruising crime scenes, one of the gang. I check the close-up of Frank Rizzo kissing a baby, the kid's mouth caught in a circle of dread. The kind of shot Franny was famous for, prize winner from the word go. Then Joey came along and the rest is misery.

"It's okay, she just woke up so she's a little groggy," he leans to whisper. "Make a fuss, could you, Rile? And don't let her see you wince."

Oh man, it's awful. Franny's barely a bump in the blankets, the rest is skull and yellow eyeballs. Not just thin but shrunken, tiny. She looks at me and wheezes a laugh.

"Riley Prentiss, as I live and breathe."

"I would have come sooner, Fran. I didn't know."

"Don't look at me, Riley. Just talk. You were always such a talker."

"I think I went off a little on Joey. Do me a favor and tell him I'm sorry."

"Joey loves me, Riley. I know it's hard to remember, but we were good together once."

"You stuck it out. That counts for something."

"Talk to me, Riley."

What can I tell her? How well everyone's doing? After burning her bridges at the *Daily News*, Franny severed all ties, shacking up with Joey in a West Philly flop. Every now and then someone would see her downtown but she'd slink off or pretend not to know you.

"I still have my Bowie tickets. Remember, Fran? He canceled and we got drunk in the Spectrum parking lot."

Her laugh rattles in her chest. "I puked into Joey's hands. Like he was gonna catch it all and take it away."

"I was glad they didn't show. I hated those things."

"I remember you'd say, 'want to get rid of all the assholes? Nuke a Rolling Stones concert.'"

Fran's breath is ragged and I can see the bones of her knuckles through her skin. I grab a chair and drag it over.

"How did so much time go by, Fran?"

"Joey says you're still with Kathleen. That's good to hear."

"You kidding? She'll never lose me now."

"I wish I'd been older . . . Who knows? I might have gotten you."

Don't want to think about that. Back when I was easy to get and up to the eyes in my own cloud of chemicals. And Joey was right about that uniform. If Kathleen hadn't snatched me up there's no telling where I'd be.

"I'm scared, Riley."

"Hey." I move to her bedside. "The Franny I knew wasn't scared of anything."

"What comes next?" She takes my hand. "What if all the crap they fed us is true? Hey, Riley, I see pearly gates and I'm fucked."

"Come on, Fran. You know what comes next."

"No, I don't. Tell me."

"It's simple." I stroke her fingers. "You wake up in a mansion and you're twenty-five years old. You have a big magic box and a smaller magic box. The big box is for the things you want that are big, the smaller one for things you want that are smaller. You use them a lot at first, but eventually you have everything you'll ever need."

"Oh Riley, let it be true."

"That's just the half of it. Everything is paid for. You can eat and drink as much as you want or not at all, as you prefer. You're never tired but you can sleep for weeks. Men adore you but you're fiercely independent. You speak perfect French."

"Make it Italian."

"Like a native. And the best part? Your time is all your own. You can write your memoirs and learn to play the drums. Or you can lie around in your pajamas watching TV all day."

"Will you come see me? You know, after you . . ."

"First thing, Franny. We'll compare notes and see how far off I was."

"I'd like that. You were the one who was always nice . . . nice guy . . ." She starts to fade.

I try to see the old Fran in her face, but there's no bringing it back. I watch until she's breathing easy then kiss her cheek and whisper good-bye. The TV's on downstairs but Joey's nowhere to be found. I slip two twenties under the sugar bowl and let myself out.

Tom Larsen has been writing fiction for twenty-five years and his work has appeared in *Newsday*, *Raritan*, *Best American Mystery Stories*, and the *LA Review*. His novels *Flawed* and *Into the Fire* are available through Amazon. Tom's wife, Andree, worked for years as a nurse on a detox unit and he has seen first-hand the ravages of addiction and the hazards of recovery.

Pledge Week

Wendy Elizabeth Ingersoll

Rain in October is a kind of weeping,
maybe at all the leaves fallen,

maybe at how I jive the other women tonight,
tell them I tidied my study, bagged and tagged,

that I shed old poems, emails from people I possibly loved
no more, that I put my life in order, this last

embroidery verging on deceit. In my study
I'd tuned the radio to hear

the voices between the fugues—pledge week,
they asked us to give what we could, even if small.

Here, tonight, everyone's come in chilled,
shaking rain from their coats. Any of them

could be my sister, any of them
  I could love —

Wendy Elizabeth Ingersoll is a retired piano teacher with five fabulous grandchildren. Her book *Grace Only Follows* won the National Federation of Press Women Contest. She has been published in *Naugatuck River Review, Connecticut River Review, Passager, Gargoyle, Main Street Rag, Mojave River Review, Delmarva Review, Broadkill Review, Worcester Review, Hartskill Review*, and Diane Lockward's *The Crafty Poet.* Her manuscript *White Crane Spreads Its Wings* was a finalist for the Dogfish Poetry Prize in 2015. She serves as a poetry reader for the *Delmarva Review.*

Acknowledgments

The editor would like to acknowledge the following:

Although this anthology is not a product of, or affiliated with, the Faces and Voices of Recovery organization, I would like to acknowledge their efforts in creating the model for Recovery Community Organizations. Without their advocacy and guidance, Recover Wyoming would not exist.

Jennifer Top of TulipTree Publishing, for her hard work in putting all the pieces of the anthology together into a real, live, miraculous book—and for her friendship most of all.

The Recover Wyoming Board of Directors, for supporting this anthology and participating in its promotion.

The writers who offered their stories and poems to this anthology—all for the princely sum of one copy. Some of them endured the poking and prodding of a pesky editor. I am incredibly grateful for their generosity, hard work, and courage.

Brian Daldorph, University of Kansas English professor, for bringing us the poetry of Shane Crady and Antonio Sanchez-Day. These poems came out of "Brian's Writing Class," which has been taking place every week since 2001 at the Douglas County Jail in Lawrence, Kansas. This creative writing class gives inmates the chance to write poems and stories, and share them with classmates. In 2008 some of this writing was published in an anthology, *Douglas County Jail Blues* (Coal City Review Press). In 2009, Brian Daldorph published his own book of poems about the class, *Jail Time* (Original Plus Press).

Laura N. Griffith, Founder and Executive Director of Recover Wyoming, for not following her little sister's advice to "just go out and find a nice little stress-free job." Instead she went big and created Recover Wyoming, a place of healing and hope. *Way to go, seester.*

Made in the USA
Middletown, DE
19 October 2016